THE SECRET IS IN
REMEMBERING

Why We Suffer, Why We Forget, and How to Return to
Who We Are

Mardoche Sidor, MD
Karen Dubin, Ph.D., LCSW
SWEET Institute

SWEET Institute Publishing
Transformational Books for a Transformational World

Published by:

SWEET Institute Publishing

New York, NY

WWW.SWEETInstitutePublishing.com

First Edition

Printed in the United States of America

ISBN (Paperback): [978-1-968105-06-8]

Library of Congress Control Number: 2025942011

Cover Design: [SWEET Institute Publishing]

Interior Design and Layout: [SWEET Institute Publishing]

For bulk orders, permissions, or media inquiries, please contact:

info@sweetinstitutepublishing.com

Unless otherwise noted, all stories and case examples in this book are either fictionalized or used with permission, and identifying details have been changed to protect the privacy of individuals.

SWEET Institute Publishing
Transformational Books for a Transformational World

Dedication

To the ones who forgot—because forgetting was once the only way to survive.

To the ones who are remembering—layer by layer, breath by breath, moment by moment.

To the clinicians, healers, guides, and companions—who hold space not just for change, but for return.

And to the remembered self within each of us—the part that was never lost, only waiting.

This book is for you.

Because the secret is—and always has been—in remembering.

Other Books by Mardoche Sidor, M.D; Karen Dubin, PhD, LCSW; with the SWEET Institute

- Journey to Empowerment

- Discovering Your Worth: Everything You Need to Feel Fulfilled

- The Power of Faith: A Harvard-Trained Psychiatrist Speaking on Faith

- The Psychotherapy Certificate Course: The Clinician and Coach Manual (Books 1–3)

- The Anxiety Course: The Workbook

- What's Missing

- NLP for Clinicians

- 50 SWEET Poems: Reflections on life, love and self

- The Power of Belief: How Ideas Shape Leaders, Nations and the Future

- The Courage to Care: Stories of Healing, Hope, and the Power of Social Work: Told by Over 50 SWEET Institute Social Workers

- Transforming Team Relationships from the Inside Out: The SWEET Healing Circle for Agencies: Redefining Accountability, Collaboration, and Culture

- Remembering: The Journey Back to the Pre-Conditioned Self

- The Clinician's Mirror: A Story of Projection, Self-Awareness, and Transformation for Clinicians

Table of Contents

Foreword

By Vilma Martinez-Gordon, LCSW

There are books we read for information, and then there are books that read us. The Secret Is in Remembering is that kind of book. As I read it—slowly, breath by breath—I didn't feel like I was learning something new. I felt like I was being reminded of something ancient. Something I had always known, but somehow forgotten. Something just beneath the surface of everything I've ever done as a clinician, and everything I've ever needed as a human being.

This book is not just theory or poetry or science. It is an experience. It moves through the conscious, the pre-conscious, the unconscious, and the existential with clarity, beauty, and integrity. It speaks to the mind, but it also speaks to the soul— and we need more of that in our field.

As a therapist, I've spent decades sitting with others in their forgetting—and in their remembering. I've seen how trauma distorts identity, how silence becomes a survival strategy, and how meaning can be lost in the very systems meant to support healing. I've also seen how one pause, one breath, one act of witnessing can open a doorway back to truth.

This book offers that doorway.

Karen and Mardoche do something rare here: they hold complexity without confusion. They offer tools without formulas. They respect both the clinical and the mystical. And most of all, they walk the path they describe—with humility, precision, and presence.

The Secret Is in Remembering isn't a quick fix or a motivational pep talk. It is a layered guide for those who are ready to live from their essence, not just their history. It is for clinicians, seekers, survivors, and anyone who knows, deep down, that there must be more to healing than symptom management. And there is.

I believe this book will not only change lives—it will change how we understand what it means to be whole.

To remember is to return. To return is to reclaim. And this book is a mirror, a map, and a prayer for that return.

May it serve you well. And may it remind you, as it reminded me: You were never broken. You only forgot.

With reverence,

By Vilma Martinez-Gordon, LCSW

Preface

By the Authors

There are books you decide to write, and then there are books that decide to be written through you. This is that kind of book. We did not set out to write a book about remembering, we set out to make sense of suffering. We've spent our lives walking with people through the darkest corridors of the human experience—through trauma, addiction, shame, despair, rage, and numbness. We've watched brilliant minds spiral, we've seen survivors' forget they survived, we've witnessed people with all the right tools still feel hollow, lost, unseen—even to themselves, and we asked: Why?

Why do we know what to do and still not do it? Why do we heal and still not feel whole? Why do we chase insight but stay in the same loop? What we came to understand—and what this book reveals—is that the true wound is not just pain. The true wound is forgetting. Forgetting who we are beneath the patterns; forgetting what we knew before the trauma. Forgetting what we came here to remember.

And so, this book was born. Not as a manual. Not as a set of strategies. But as a pathway back.

Back to breath. Back to identity. Back to truth. We wrote this for our clients, our colleagues, our community—but also for ourselves. For the parts of us that forgot. For the versions of us that performed, produced, pushed through. For the younger selves that learned survival was safer than selfhood. And for the parts that began to whisper… there's more.

This book honors that whisper. It listens. It guides. It breathes. We wrote it for clinicians tired of symptom-chasing. We wrote it for the ones who feel like healing is working—but something is still missing. We wrote it for the overachievers, the caretakers, the seekers, the skeptics.

We wrote it for the ones who made it through, but never felt like they arrived.

We wrote it for you. This is not a book about becoming. It is a book about returning. Through the conscious. Through the pre-conscious. Through the unconscious. And through the precious layer no one taught us how to name: the existential.

The layer of meaning.

The layer of essence.

The layer where healing ends and truth begins.

So, as you turn these pages, we ask you to do what the world rarely gives us permission to do:

Pause.

Breathe.

Listen.

Not to us—but to the part of you that already knows.

Because the secret is not in striving, fixing, or even healing.

The secret is in remembering.

With devotion,

Mardoche Sidor, M.D.
Karen Dubin, Ph.D., LCSW
New York City
Spring 2025

Introduction

Why We Forget—and Why We Must Remember

You're here for a reason.

Not just in this moment, holding this book.

But here—in this life, in this body, in this season of your becoming.

You've done the work.

You've read the books.

You've shown up for therapy.

You've tried mindfulness, routines, healing plans, breathing strategies, even surrender.

And yet… something still feels missing.

It's not that you're broken.

It's not that you're lazy or resistant or lacking willpower.

It's that you're still trying to solve a spiritual wound with behavioral tools alone.

Because what hurts the most—what haunts, sabotages, exhausts, and isolates us—is not just trauma.

It's not just dysfunction, anxiety, depression, addiction, or grief.

It's the loss of identity that comes with forgetting who we are.

This Is the Hidden Root of Suffering

We don't suffer because we haven't read the right book, taken the right course, or found the perfect therapist.

We suffer because we've forgotten something essential:

- Who we were before the world told us who to be.
- What we knew before we were taught to survive.
- The self we buried in order to belong.

And when we forget, we start living from scripts, defenses, roles, and routines. We chase success but feel empty. We develop insight but still feel stuck. We heal symptoms but never quite feel whole.

This book exists because that is no longer acceptable.

This Is Not a Self-Help Book

This is not about becoming a better version of yourself.

This is about returning to what is already true.

It is a journey inward—layer by layer—through the very architecture of your being:

- Conscious Layer – The behaviors, habits, and choices you control
- Pre-Conscious Layer – The patterns and beliefs that whisper below awareness
- Unconscious Layer – The repressed stories, memories, and symbols shaping your life
- Existential Layer – The deepest layer of all: your essence, meaning, and identity

When we ignore these layers, we live fragmented lives.

When we remember them—we integrate, we awaken, we return.

Who This Book Is For

- It's for clinicians and healers who are tired of surface-level models and long for depth.

- It's for overachievers, overthinkers, and caretakers who have mastered doing, but forgotten how to be.

- It's for those who have survived—but haven't yet returned to themselves.

- It's for anyone who senses, deep down: There is more. And I am ready.

You will move through this book not just by reading—but by experiencing.

Each chapter includes:

- A clinical insight grounded in science

- A real-world dialogue or moment of reflection

- A transformational tool or practice

- A question to anchor your remembering

- And a way to integrate it—not just in your mind, but in your body, breath, and choices

This is not information for your head.

This is an invitation to your whole self.

This Is the Work of Our Time

In a world that rewards forgetting—forgetting rest, truth, selfhood, community, meaning—remembering is a radical act.

It is also a precious one.

To remember is not just to think back.

It is to re-member—to become whole again.

And this book is here to walk with you—

Through every layer.

Through every pause.

Through every breath back home.

Because:

You were never lost.

You only forgot.

And now—

you are ready to remember.

Why This Book

Because we've seen it too many times.

The brilliant clinician who loses themselves in caregiving.

The trauma survivor who knows all the theories but still feels unworthy.

The spiritual seeker who tries every tool but can't explain the ache.

The person with insight, stability, and even joy—who still senses… something is missing.

That missing thing isn't knowledge.

It's not motivation.

It's not another certification, another journal prompt, another retreat.

What's missing is remembering.

Remembering who we are beneath the defenses, beneath the diagnoses, beneath the roles we perform and the expectations we carry.

This book was written because in our work—in clinical sessions, community healing, breathwork groups, moments of silence— we kept witnessing the same moment:

That pause when someone stops performing, stops trying to be good, and suddenly says something that doesn't come from the intellect—it comes from the soul.

That is the moment of remembering.

It is precious. It is real. It changes everything.

And it is what we are here to recover.

This book is not here to give you more to do.

It is here to give you a path home.

To the self you lost.

The part you silenced.

The truth you buried under survival.

We wrote this book because:

- Healing is not to be a race or a performance.
- Clinical work is not to end at symptom relief.
- Identity is not to be left out of the treatment plan.
- Suffering is not to be pathologized when it is, in fact, precious.
- Remembering is not to be reserved for the privileged few who stumble into it by accident.

This book is here to systematize the precious, to make wholeness practical, and to return you to yourself—not just once, but as a rhythm.

Because the world needs people who remember who they are.

People who can lead from alignment, not fear.

People who can listen without ego.

People who can rest without shame.

People who can say: I know who I am. I remember.

That is why this book exists.

That is why you're holding it now.

Not by chance.

But because the part of you that never forgot…

is ready to be seen.

What This Book Is About

This book is about remembering who you are—beneath the noise, beneath the patterns, beneath the survival.

It is about why we suffer, not just because of trauma or loss or stress—but because we have forgotten something essential.

Forgotten the truth of who we are.

Forgotten what we once knew, before we had to protect ourselves.

Forgotten how to listen—not just to the world, but to the self beneath the performance.

This book is about reclaiming that truth, through a four-layered framework that integrates science, soul, story, and self:

The Four Layers of Remembering:

1. Conscious Layer – Behavior, choice, routines, language
2. Pre-Conscious Layer – Schemas, emotional patterns, internal dialogue
3. Unconscious Layer – Repression, symbols, dreams, body memory
4. Existential Layer – Identity, essence, meaning, soul

Each chapter is an entry point into one of these layers.

Each tool is designed to activate insight and integration.

Each practice invites you not just to understand—but to embody.

This book is about transformation—not by force, but by return.

It is not about adding more.

It is about subtracting what is not true.

It is about becoming deeply familiar with the rhythms of your own soul.

It is also a book for clinicians, helpers, and healers.

Because if we are to walk people home to themselves, we must first remember our own path.

This book gives language, structure, and tools to guide others through behavioral change, belief deconstruction, symbolic integration, and existential alignment.

It is evidence-based.

It is soul-honoring.

It is practical, poetic, and powerful.

Above all, this book is about one thing:

Remembering what we already know, so we can live like we never forgot.

How This Book Works

A Layered Journey from Forgetting to Integration

This book is not linear.

It's layered.

Because you are not linear.

Your healing isn't either.

We've organized the book according to the four layers of remembering—each building on the previous one, each inviting you deeper into yourself.

The Structure

The book is divided into five parts:

1. Part I: The Suffering of Forgetting

Why we struggle, why we disconnect, and the invisible cost of living out of alignment.

2. Part II: The Four Layers of Remembering

A deep dive into the conscious, pre-conscious, unconscious, and existential aspects of transformation.

3. Part III: Remembering Through Time

How memory, trauma, early development, and even pre-birth experience shape who we believe we are—and how to begin again.

4. Part IV: The Shift

What happens when we remember. How life changes. How trust, presence, and meaning return.

5. Part V: Integration

Daily practices, tools, precious pauses, and rituals to make remembering a way of life.

The Flow of Each Chapter

To make the book experiential and integrative, each chapter includes:

- Opening Quote or Poetic Frame – to ground you in theme
- A Dialogue or Vignette – to make it real
- Scientific Insight – so you understand the why
- A Tool or Practice – so you can apply the work
- Reflection Prompt – to deepen your awareness
- Clinical Integration – for those guiding others through this process
- Suggested Weekly Action – so remembering becomes embodied, not just understood

You Can Read This Two Ways

1. Chronologically – as a complete arc, moving layer by layer
2. Intuitively – choosing the chapter that speaks to where you are right now

You'll know which to follow. Your remembering already began the moment you opened this book.

For Clinicians and Healers

This book can be used in therapy, supervision, group work, and healing circles.

The tools are science-based and fidelity-friendly. The practices are adaptable to diverse populations. And the existential framework gives you a vocabulary for the kind of work most training programs never taught you to name.

You don't have to do this work alone. This book is your companion.

One Final Note on Process

You may want to rush.

You may want to underline everything.

You may want to intellectualize your way to clarity.

Instead, we invite you to breathe.

Pause.

Feel.

Let the words enter your cells, not just your mind.

Because this book doesn't just describe remembering.

It helps you live it.

How to Use This Book

From Information to Integration

This book is not meant to be read passively.

It is meant to be lived.

You will not find a step-by-step formula. You will find a pathway—layered, cyclical, and designed for remembering the self beneath conditioning, trauma, and habit.

To make the most of this journey, here's how we recommend you engage:

1. Don't rush.

This book was written slowly, to be read slowly.

You may want to move chapter by chapter, or linger in one section for days or weeks. That's not stalling—that's integration.

2. Follow the structure.

Each chapter includes:

- A quote or entry to center the theme
- A dialogue or clinical moment to ground the work in reality
- A scientific insight to explain the why
- A transformational tool or practice
- A reflection prompt to deepen awareness
- A clinical integration section (especially for practitioners)
- A weekly suggestion for embodied application

These are not extras. They are part of the remembering process.

3. Make it yours.

Use the margins. Pause for the questions. Revisit the rituals. Return to a tool you thought you understood and let it work on a new level of you.

This book is written for you—and also with you.

4. Bring your body.

Remembering is not an intellectual act.

It lives in breath.

In sensation.

In rhythm.

In presence.

Breathe often.

Stretch.

Pause.

Notice how your body responds to what you read.

5. Use the Toolkit and Appendices.

At the end of the book, you'll find the Reader Integration Toolkit, Visual Tools, Precious Pause Practices, and other appendices designed to support your daily application. Use them. Adapt them. Share them.

6. Don't do this alone.

This work is precious—but it is also communal. Share your journey with others. Use this book in peer groups, clinical supervision, healing circles, or with trusted companions. There is remembering we cannot do until we are witnessed.

7. When in doubt, pause.

If you ever feel overwhelmed, stuck, activated, or unsure what to do next…

Pause.

Return to your breath.

Turn to a page that anchors you.

Whisper: I am still remembering.

That's enough.

This book isn't asking you to become something more.

It's inviting you to uncover what's already within.

Let it be a mirror.

Let it be a rhythm.

Let it be a return.

Front Acknowledgments

This book would not exist without a community of minds, hearts, and hands—each of whom contributed in ways both seen and unseen.

To our editorial and design collaborators at SWEET Institute Publishing, thank you for holding the vision and guiding every detail to completion.

To the researchers, scholars, and scientists whose work bridges memory, meaning, and healing—your insights laid the groundwork for what we've built here.

To our colleagues, clinical teams, and mentors, thank you for your feedback, encouragement, and shared belief that remembering is not only possible, but necessary.

To the many readers, early reviewers, and SWEET community members who sat with drafts, asked questions, and reminded us why this message matters—thank you for helping us shape this book with clarity and care.

To our families—thank you for the patience, love, and presence that allowed us to write, revise, and remember.

And to every teacher who came before us, in voice or in silence, in pain or in wisdom—you are acknowledged here, and always.

With appreciation,

Karen Dubin, Ph.D., LCSW
Mardoche Sidor, M.D.
All remembering is relational—nothing is remembered alone.

Part I: The Suffering of Forgetting

Chapter 1: The Illusion of Should

Why We Do What We're Not Meant to Do—
And Suffer Because of It

I know what I should be doing, she said. And yet, she wasn't doing it. Not because she was lazy, not because she was undisciplined. But because deep down, it wasn't hers to do.

Our deepest suffering doesn't come from failing to do what we think we should — it comes from believing we have to do it in the first place.

— Karen Dubin, Ph.D., LCSW

The Dialogue

Patient: I keep setting goals. Meditate daily. Exercise more. Eat clean. But I sabotage it every time. I just don't get it.

Clinician: What happens when you don't follow through?

Patient: I feel shame. I compare myself to everyone on Instagram. And then I spiral. I feel like a failure.

Clinician: Could it be that you're not failing—but instead, being pulled toward something more true?

Patient: But I should be doing those things.

Clinician: Says who?

And there it is.

The **Conditioned Self** speaking through the word should.

Level One: The Conscious Layer

This is the level of action—what we do, how we behave, the habits we form.

And at this level, the illusion of should dominates.

We read self-help books. We create lists. We chase routines.

But we rarely pause to ask:

Is this what I truly want—or just what I've been told I should want?

Scientific Insight:

Studies show that behavior change fails not because of poor willpower, but because of misalignment with intrinsic motivation (Ryan & Deci, 2000). Behavior driven by external shoulds— social norms, peer comparison, cultural scripts—activates avoidance motivation, which increases stress and cortisol (Muraven et al., 1998).

The Should Audit Tool

The Should Audit Tool ("The Illusion of 'Should'") is designed to help readers and clients:

- Identify inherited, imposed, or conditioned "shoulds"
- Examine the emotional, behavioral, and existential cost of these "shoulds"
- Begin to untangle what is authentic from what is expected
- Move from unconscious obligation to conscious choice

Step 1: List Your "Shoulds"

Write down 10–15 of your most common 'should' statements— across all areas: work, family, identity, body, emotions, relationships, success, etc.

Example: "I should be more productive." "I should be married by now."

Step 2: Source Each "Should"

For each, ask:

- Where did this come from? (Culture, family, religion, education, media, trauma?)
- Who benefits if I believe and follow this?
- Who am I trying not to disappoint?

Step 3: Emotional Inventory

Reflect on each "should":

- How does this make me feel when I believe it?
- Inspired or trapped?
- Motivated or guilty?
- Empowered or ashamed?

Step 4: The Truth Beneath

Now challenge the "should" by asking:

- What if this isn't true?
- What do I want, believe, or value?
- What would I do or feel if I released this?

Step 5: Reframe or Release

Transform the "should" into:

- A choice ("I choose to…")
- A value-based want ("I value connection, so I'm choosing…")
- Or, release it entirely

Scientific Insight

Cognitive behavioral research has long shown that rigid beliefs, especially "should" or "must" statements, are associated with:

- Higher levels of anxiety and depression (Beck, 1979)
- Increased shame, guilt, and chronic dissatisfaction
- Cognitive distortions like demandingness, all-or-nothing thinking, and catastrophizing

Replacing "should" statements with flexible, values-aligned language is a core principle of Rational Emotive Behavior Therapy (REBT) (Ellis, 1962) and ACT (Acceptance and Commitment Therapy).

Clinical Integration

Use the Should Audit Tool:

- With clients who present with guilt, pressure, internal conflict
- In identity work, trauma recovery, self-compassion interventions
- As a homework assignment, journaling prompt, or session starter

SHOULD AUDIT TOOL

ACTIVITY	WHY DO I THINK I SHOULD DO THIS?	IS THIS TRULY ALIGNED WITH ME?	IF NOT, WHAT IS?
MEDITATE EVERY MORNING	It's what all spiritual people do.	Maybe. But I hate sitting still.	I love walking in silence.
GET A PROMOTION	It's what success looks like.	No. I value flexibility more.	Build a consulting practice.

Reflection Prompt:

List 5 things you keep saying you should do.

Now ask: Who told me I should do this?

Then Ask: And more importantly, do I choose this, from a place of remembering who I am?

Level Two: The Preconscious Layer

Here we find our schemas—unconscious patterns, internalized beliefs, and default scripts from early experiences.

Common schemas (are these schemas or statements that point to our schemas) that fuel the illusion of should:

- If I don't succeed, I'm not worthy.

- Others will reject me unless I perform.

- There is a right way to be.

Modality Integration:

- Schema Therapy: helps identify and re-script these maladaptive beliefs (Young et al., 2003)

- ACT (Acceptance and Commitment Therapy): helps defuse from these beliefs and return to values (Hayes et al., 1999)

Try This: Thought Defusion Practice

Say the thought: I should be doing more.

Now say: I'm having the thought that I should be doing more.

Now: I notice I'm having the thought that I should be doing more.

Feel the space grow.

Level Three: The Unconscious Layer

Here lies the origin of the should.

Buried beneath awareness is the child who once heard:

You're too much.

You'll only be loved if…

You're not enough.

Repression and the Ideal Self

Freud spoke of the ego-ideal—a part of us formed by parental and societal expectations, always judging, always demanding (Freud, 1914).

We internalize it, forget its origin, and mistake it for truth.

Technique: Free Association

Take a quiet moment.

Write down I should…

Now keep writing without censoring.

Let the unconscious speak.

What memories come up? Whose voice is speaking?

Integration Across the Three Levels

Layer	Intervention	Key Insight	Practical Tool
Conscious	Behavior Audit	Not all action is alignment	Not all action is alignment
Preconscious	Schema Work	My shoulds come from scripts	My shoulds come from scripts
Unconscious	Free Association	The voice isn't mine	The voice isn't mine

Behavior Audit Tool

The Behavior Audit is a structured self-assessment designed to help identify automatic behaviors rooted in internalized 'shoulds,' unconscious beliefs, and forgotten emotional patterns. It supports the reader in connecting their daily actions to deeper psychological layers—conscious, preconscious, and unconscious.

Instructions

Use this audit to explore the behaviors you perform daily or habitually. For each behavior, complete the five reflection steps below.

Behavior Reflection Steps:

1. Behavior Description
2. Inner Command (e.g., 'I should...', 'I have to...')
3. Source (Fear, Comparison, Trauma, Approval-seeking, etc.)
4. Topographical Layer (Conscious, Preconscious, Unconscious)
5. Alignment: Does this reflect who I truly am?

Behavior Audit Template

BEHAVIOR	INNER COMMAND	SOURCE	TOPOGRAPHICAL LAYER	IS THIS ALIGNED WITH MY TRUTH?
				✖ ✔

Commitment Practice: The Reclamation List

Each morning this week, write:

1. One should I'm letting go of today
2. One truth I'm reclaiming about who I am

Example:

- Letting go: I should hustle nonstop
- Reclaiming: I create best when I rest

In Summary

We suffer not because we are off track, but because we are on someone else's track.

We forget our truth and follow the noise.

But the secret is in remembering:

We were never meant to follow the should.

We were meant to follow the precious.

References

- Deci, E. L., & Ryan, R. M. (2000). The what and why of goal pursuits: Human needs and the self-determination of behavior. Psychological Inquiry, 11(4), 227–268.

- Muraven, M., Tice, D. M., & Baumeister, R. F. (1998). Self-control as limited resource: Regulatory depletion patterns. Journal of Personality and Social Psychology, 74(3), 774–789.

- Young, J. E., Klosko, J. S., & Weishaar, M. E. (2003). Schema therapy: A practitioner's guide.

- Hayes, S. C., Strosahl, K. D., & Wilson, K. G. (1999). Acceptance and commitment therapy: An experiential approach to behavior change.

- Freud, S. (1914). On narcissism: An introduction.

Chapter 2: The Mirror of Comparison

The Pain of Measuring Ourselves by the Standards of Others

Comparison is the thief of joy, said Roosevelt. But what if it's more than that? What if comparison is the thief of truth? The thief of peace? The thief of the self?

Comparison is not about who they are. It's about what we forgot about ourselves.

— Mardoche Sidor, MD

The Dialogue

Clinician: What's been making things harder lately?

Patient: Everyone else seems to be doing better. They're getting married. Buying homes. Launching businesses. Meanwhile, I'm… lost.

Clinician: Do you think they feel as certain inside as they appear outside?

Patient: Maybe not. But still… I just don't measure up.

Clinician: To whom? And according to what?

Patient: I don't even know anymore.

This is the crisis of comparison.

A quiet epidemic—dissatisfaction, self-doubt, and despair—rooted in a simple forgetting: That our paths are preciously, necessarily different.

Level One: The Conscious Layer

At the conscious level, comparison is visible in our behaviors and reactions:

- Scrolling social media, feeling inferior
- Overworking to catch up
- Mimicking others' goals
- Dismissing our own desires

Scientific Insight:

Research shows that upward social comparison (comparing ourselves to those we perceive as better off) is linked to depressive symptoms and lower self-esteem (Appel et al., 2016; Vogel et al., 2014).

Cognitive Distortion Alert:

Comparison often leads to Selective Attention Bias—we notice others' highlight reels and ignore their struggles.

This activates the default mode network in our brains, fueling rumination and imagined inadequacy.

The Comparison Journal

Purpose:

To transform unconscious comparison into conscious self-connection.

Instructions:

For at least 7 consecutive days, use the journal daily. At the end of each day (or during the day if possible), reflect and write down:

1. When did I compare myself to someone else today?
2. (Be specific: who, where, when?)
3. What was the effect on my thoughts, emotions, or behaviors?
4. (Did it make me feel inadequate, superior, motivated, disconnected?)
5. What belief about myself was triggered by this comparison?
6. (E.g., "I'm not successful," "I'm falling behind," "I'm not lovable.")
7. Where do I think that belief comes from?
8. (Reflect briefly: early life, culture, social media?)
9. What truth can I anchor into instead?
10. (E.g., "My path is unique," "I'm allowed to grow at my pace," "I am already enough.")
11. What action can I take to reconnect with myself?
12. (Something small: breath, movement, gratitude, writing, silence, calling someone.)
13. Bonus Prompt (End of Week):

    - "What do I learn about myself when I compare myself to others?"

    - "What would it feel like to live free from comparison— even for a day?"

MOMENT OF COMPARISON	WHO/WHAT WAS I COMPARING?	WHAT DID I FEEL?	WHAT DID I FORGET ABOUT MYSELF?
SAW FRIEND'S BOOK LAUNCH	I HAVEN'T PUBLISHED YET	INADEQUATE, BEHIND	I'M WRITING SOMETHING THAT MATTERS DEEPLY.

Reflection Prompt:

Today, when I feel less than, I will pause and ask:

What have I forgotten about myself in this moment?

Level Two: The Preconscious Layer

At the preconscious level, comparison stems from core beliefs formed in childhood and reinforced over time:

- I'm not enough.
- There's one right path.
- Success looks like X.
- I need to prove I matter.

Modality Integration

- Attachment Theory: Early caregivers shape our internal sense of worth and validation-seeking.
- Schema Therapy: Comparison is often rooted in the Defectiveness or Unrelenting Standards schemas.

Schema Mapping Tool

Purpose:

The Schema Mapping Tool is designed to help readers identify, trace, and begin to shift the internalized beliefs and comparison-driven thought patterns that influence their self-image and behavior. This tool encourages awareness of how deeply rooted schemas shape their relationships, decisions, and sense of worth.

Instructions:

1. Choose a recent situation where you found yourself comparing your life, body, intelligence, success, or relationship to someone else's.

2. Write out:

    a. The Situation

    b. The Automatic Thought or Feeling

    c. The Underlying Belief or Schema:

    d. Where You Think That Schema Originated (e.g., childhood, culture, school, media):

3. Identify what emotion is attached to this schema (shame, fear, inadequacy, etc.).

4. Reflect

    a. Is this schema accurate, helpful, or serving your growth?

5. Counterbalance

    a. What new belief could you choose instead? What evidence supports this new belief?

Example:

- **Situation**: I saw a colleague announce a promotion on LinkedIn.

- **Automatic Thought**: 'I'll never be that successful.'

- **Underlying Schema**: 'I'm always behind.'

- **Origin**: Grew up being compared to siblings.

- **Emotion**: Insecurity and inadequacy.

- **Counter Belief**: 'My path is unique, and I'm building something meaningful in my own way.'

- **Evidence**: Feedback from clients, past successes, aligned values.

Reflection Prompts:

- What patterns of comparison show up most often in your inner dialogue?

- Which schemas feel the oldest? Which ones feel the most powerful?

- If you were free of these comparison schemas, how would your choices, relationships, and self-talk shift?

Try This: Schema Mapping Exercise

Choose one moment of painful comparison.

Ask: What belief got activated? Whose voice is that?

Then: What new voice do I want to remember today?

Level Three: The Unconscious Layer

At the unconscious level, comparison may be a defense—a mask over something deeper:

- A repressed fear of not being seen
- A longing to be loved for who we are, not what we achieve
- A forgotten grief of abandonment or invisibility

Free Association Practice:

Start with the sentence:

- I feel behind because…

Let your hand write without judgment.

What memory surfaces?

What emotion have you buried?

Freud's Insight:

The unconscious expresses itself through displacement—we attack ourselves over surface-level differences instead of confronting deeper wounds.

Integration Across the Three Levels

Layer	Intervention	Key Insight	Practice/Tool
Conscious	Comparison Journal	I forget my own worth when I compare	Reflection & Reframing Prompts
Preconscious	Schema Identification	I internalized false standards	Schema Mapping Exercise
Unconscious	Free Association	Comparison covers deeper pain	Repressed Memory Inquiry

Integration Across the Three Levels

The Mirror Reset – Commitment Practice

The Mirror Reset is a daily commitment practice designed to interrupt internalized comparison, judgment, and self-criticism. It invites you to re-see yourself—not through the lens of others, but through the truth of who you are.

Why the 'Mirror'

The mirror is both literal and symbolic. We use it to see ourselves daily, often to evaluate or criticize. This practice transforms the mirror into a space of self-recognition and compassion.

Why the 'Reset'

The reset refers to a re-patterning of your neural pathways. By speaking truth aloud, making eye contact with yourself, and engaging in this daily ritual, you reset the mental and emotional script you've inherited or adopted.

Instructions for the Mirror Reset

1. Stand in front of a mirror.
2. Make direct eye contact with yourself.
3. Say aloud a statement of remembering. Example: 'I am enough. I am not who they told me I had to be. I am who I remember myself to be.'
4. Repeat 3–5 times, slowly, until you feel a shift in your body or mind.
5. Do this daily, especially when you feel self-doubt, shame, or comparison creeping in.

Scientific Insight

Research shows that mirror exposure and positive affirmations can reduce cortisol levels and increase oxytocin, enhancing emotional regulation and self-compassion (Delinsky & Wilson,

2006; Creswell et al., 2013). Daily repetition builds new neural pathways through the brain's natural neuroplasticity.

This practice is not about perfection—it's about presence. Let the mirror be a space of returning, each day, to the truth of who you are.

Each night this week, write:

1. One moment I compared myself today

2. What I remembered about myself instead

Example:

- **Compared**: My friend just had a baby.

- **Remembered**: My path is unfolding perfectly. I am preparing life in a different way.

In Summary

Comparison is not the problem.

It's the symptom.

The problem is forgetting who we are.

When we remember, we stop competing with others and start collaborating with life.

We stop chasing borrowed dreams and start honoring the deep script already written within us.

The mirror doesn't lie.

It just reflects who we think we are.

When we clear the fog, we see:

- We were never behind. We were never less. We were never late.

- We were becoming.

References

- Appel, H., Gerlach, A. L., & Crusius, J. (2016). The interplay between Facebook use, social comparison, envy, and depression. Current Opinion in Psychology, 9, 44–49.

- Vogel, E. A., Rose, J. P., Roberts, L. R., & Eckles, K. (2014). Social comparison, social media, and self-esteem. Psychology of Popular Media Culture, 3(4), 206–222.

- Young, J. E., Klosko, J. S., & Weishaar, M. E. (2003). Schema therapy: A practitioner's guide.

- Freud, S. (1901). The psychopathology of everyday life.

- Bowlby, J. (1988). A secure base: Parent-child attachment and healthy human development.

Chapter 3: The Noise of the World and the Stillness Within

Why We Can't Hear Ourselves Anymore—And
How to Find Our Way Back

All of humanity's problems stem from man's inability to sit quietly in a room alone.

— Blaise Pascal

And yet, we rarely try.

Because the moment we slow down,

the world speeds up.

Notifications. Deadlines. Opinions.

News cycles. Algorithmic suggestions.

The pressure to respond. To perform. To stay visible.

We live in a constant hum.

A collective background noise we've confused for truth.

The Dialogue

Clinician: When was the last time you were truly alone with yourself—no phone, no music, no tasks?

Patient: (laughs nervously) I don't think I ever am. Even when I'm in bed, my mind is racing.

Clinician: What do you think might happen if you sat in silence?

Patient: I'm afraid I'll feel…empty. Or worse—like I'll have to face something I've buried.

Clinician: So, the noise helps keep it buried?

Patient: (pause) I guess…it keeps me from remembering.

And there it is again:

The fear of stillness—because in the stillness, we might meet ourselves.

Level One: The Conscious Layer

At the conscious level, noise shows up as:

- Multitasking
- Background media (music, podcasts, TV)
- Constant checking (email, news, texts)
- Loud environments (both literal and mental)

Scientific Insight:

Chronic exposure to digital and environmental noise activates the sympathetic nervous system, increasing cortisol and reducing capacity for reflective thinking (Small et al., 2020). Cognitive overload reduces working memory and emotional regulation (Ophir et al., 2009).

Noise is not just external—it becomes internal.

We forget what it feels like to be quiet.

The Silence Inventory — Tool Overview

Purpose:

To help the reader (or client) identify where, when, and how silence is either present, feared, or missing in their life—and what that reveals about their inner state, identity, and beliefs.

Instructions:

1. Scan Your Life for Silence.

- Write down when and where you regularly experience silence. Examples:

- Morning coffee?
- Evening commute?
- In conversation with others?
- During therapy?

2. Identify Discomfort with Silence.

List moments when silence feels uncomfortable, awkward, or threatening. Ask:

- Do I fill silence with noise (music, TV, talking, phone)?
- When do I avoid silence?
- What am I afraid will come up if I stay quiet?

3. Explore the Meaning of Silence.

Reflect on what silence has meant in your life:

- Was it a punishment? (e.g., silent treatment)
- A refuge?
- A threat?
- A spiritual opening?

4. Silence and Identity.

Answer:

- What does my relationship with silence say about how I see myself?
- Who am I without the noise?
- What becomes louder in me when the world goes quiet?

5. Commit to a Moment of Silence.

Choose one moment daily (start with 2–5 minutes) to be fully still and silent. No agenda. Just observe. Keep a brief journal after each session.

What It Reveals:

This tool helps surface unconscious patterns of avoidance, fear, identity over-identification, or over-stimulation—inviting the user back to presence. It serves as a bridge from outer noise to inner knowing.

TIME OF DAY	NOISE INPUT	NEEDED OR AVOIDED	ALTERNATIVE
MORNING COMMUTE	Podcast	Avoiding Being Alone With Thoughts	Try Silence of Breath Awareness
DINNER	TV in Background	Habitual	Try Soft Lighting And Chewing Slowly
BEDTIME	Scrolling Social Media	Numbing Anxiety	Try Journaling or Breath Counting

Reflection Prompt:

What am I using noise to avoid feeling?

Level Two: The Preconscious Layer

Here lies the belief:

- Stillness is unsafe.
- Slowness is weakness.
- Rest is laziness.
- If I stop, I'll fall behind.

These beliefs were often learned early in life—from families that equated worth with achievement, from schools that rewarded constant output, from cultures that confuse busyness with value.

Modality Integration:

- **ACT**: Teaches us to make space for discomfort without running from it

- **Mindfulness-Based Cognitive Therapy (MBCT):** Helps observe thoughts as events, not facts

- **Gestalt**: Encourages staying present with what arises

Practice: Contacting the Present Moment

- Sit for 60 seconds.

- Notice five things you can hear.

- Then four things you can see.

- Then three things you can feel.

- Then two things you can smell.

- Then one thing you're grateful for.

You just remembered how to come home.

Level Three: The Unconscious Layer

Stillness threatens the unconscious because it opens the door to what was repressed.

- Abandonment

- Guilt

- Loss

- Longing

- Shame

In the noise, these things stay buried.

But in the quiet, they rise.

This is why so many fear meditation—not because it doesn't work, but because it does.

Freud's Insight:

In Beyond the Pleasure Principle (1920), Freud suggested that trauma can create a compulsion to avoid stillness, as stillness reactivates unprocessed pain.

Jung's Contribution:

Jung saw stillness as the path to the Self—but only if one is willing to descend into the shadow first.

Free Association Prompt: The Unheard Voice

Write:

If I sat in complete silence for one hour, I'm afraid I might…

Then let your hand move.

No edits. No filters.

What part of you have you been avoiding?

Integration Across the Three Levels of Remembering

To truly access the stillness within, we must quiet the noise across all layers of our psychological experience. Below are three interventions—each aligned with one of the three levels of remembering—to guide the reader or clinician in this integrative work.

1. Conscious Layer: The Noise Inventory

Purpose: To raise awareness of the external and internal distractions actively present in one's daily life.

Tool: The Noise Inventory (checklist + reflection worksheet)

Practice: Track and categorize daily sources of noise (digital, emotional, social, physical), and note their impact on presence and inner peace.

Goal: To reclaim agency by consciously reducing avoidable noise.

2. Preconscious Layer: The Unheard Voice Prompt

Purpose: To uncover semi-conscious beliefs, feelings, and needs that are subtly drowned out.

Tool: The Unheard Voice Prompt (journaling or therapeutic dialogue prompt)

Practice: Respond to the question: "What part of me have I been ignoring because the world around me was too loud?"

Goal: To restore connection with intuitive or authentic inner guidance.

3. Unconscious Layer: Shadow Listening

Purpose: To access disowned or repressed material that unconsciously contributes to noise.

Tool: Shadow Listening (adapted from shadow work, includes visualization or deep inquiry)

Practice: In stillness, ask: "Whose voice is this? What part of me does it threaten or silence?" Use dream journaling, therapist-guided exploration, or body-based awareness.

Goal: To transmute hidden drivers of internal noise into wisdom and peace.

Integration Across the Three Levels

Layer	Intervention	Insight	Tool
Conscious	Noise inventory & behavior shift	Noise hides us from ourselves	Silence Inventory Table
Preconscious	Belief re-evaluation	I've been taught to fear stillness	Contacting the Present Moment
Unconscious	Free association & shadow work	Stillness reveals the hidden self	The Unheard Voice Prompt

Commitment Practice: The Precious Pause

Each day this week, commit to one precious pause:

- No phone.
- No noise.
- Just you and your breath.

Start with 3 minutes.

Then 5.

Then 10.

Then more, if you're willing.

Journal Prompt After Each Pause:

What arose? What did I feel? What did I remember?

In Summary

The world is loud.

But our soul whispers.

To hear it, we must dare to enter silence.

We must remember how to be still—not as punishment, but as path.

Because in the stillness, we hear the original song.

The one we forgot.

The one we came here to remember.

References

- Small, G., Lee, J., Kaufman, A., & Siddarth, P. (2020). Digital media use and brain development in children. JAMA Pediatrics.

- Ophir, E., Nass, C., & Wagner, A. D. (2009). Cognitive control in media multitaskers. Proceedings of the National Academy of Sciences, 106(37), 15583–15587.

- Hayes, S. C., Strosahl, K. D., & Wilson, K. G. (1999). Acceptance and Commitment Therapy.

- Segal, Z. V., Williams, J. M. G., & Teasdale, J. D. (2018). Mindfulness-based cognitive therapy for depression.

- Freud, S. (1920). Beyond the Pleasure Principle.

- Jung, C. G. (1963). Memories, Dreams, Reflections.

Part II: The Four Layers of Remembering

Chapter 4: Conscious Remembering

Awakening Through Action—The First
Doorway to Who We Are

*You do not think your way into a new way of living. You
live your way into a new way of thinking.*

— Richard Rohr

Before we can remember the deep things—

the lost things,

the ancient things,

the precious things—

we must start here:

with the conscious.

Not theory.

Not memory.

Action.

Because movement reveals identity.

And behavior becomes belief.

The Dialogue

Clinician: You keep saying you don't know who you are.

Patient: Because I don't. I feel disconnected.

Clinician: Then don't start by thinking. Start by moving.

Patient: Toward what?

Clinician: Toward the things that make you feel most alive.
Most honest. Most clear.

Patient: But I don't feel alive doing anything anymore.

Clinician: Then we start simple. Breath. Body. Structure. Stillness. Rhythm. This is how remembering begins.

Level One: The Conscious Layer

This is the surface—but not the superficial.

The conscious mind is where change begins.

It's where neuroplasticity gets activated.

It's where the brain rewires through repetition, feedback, and intention.

The conscious level includes:

- Behavior
- Habits
- Routines
- Goals
- Effort
- Sleep, food, movement
- Breath, posture, presence

It also includes what we consume:

Media. Environments. Relationships. Beliefs.

Scientific Insight

Neuroplasticity—the brain's ability to reorganize and form new connections—is strongest when we combine:

1. Intentional behavior (goal-directed action)
2. Emotionally significant feedback
3. Repetition over time

(Doidge, 2007; Kays et al., 2012)

This means we don't just think our way into remembering.

We must live it.

Routinely.

Ritually.

Relationally.

Tool: The Conscious Remembering Inventory

This inventory is designed to help you become more aware of the moments when you are aligned—or misaligned—with your deepest truth. Use it to track your behaviors, beliefs, and emotional patterns with conscious attention. Awareness is the first step to remembering.

Instructions

1. Set aside 10–15 minutes at the end of your day.
2. Reflect honestly on your day's events, emotions, and internal dialogue.
3. Answer the questions below without judgment—just awareness.
4. Complete this inventory daily for at least one week.
5. Review your entries at the end of the week and notice patterns or shifts.

Inventory Questions

1. In what moments today did I feel most like myself?
2. When did I act from a sense of 'should' rather than truth?
3. Did I speak, think, or act in ways that contradicted my inner knowing?
4. What beliefs guided my actions today—were they conscious or inherited?

5. What moment stands out as most meaningful or aligned with who I am becoming?

6. What moment stands out as most misaligned or disconnected from my truth?

7. What did I do today that I would like to continue doing tomorrow?

8. What would I like to do differently tomorrow—and why?

Reflection Prompt

What am I learning about myself through this practice of daily conscious remembering?

AREA OF LIFE	CURRENT PATTERN	DOES IT REFLECT WHO I TRULY AM?	NEW CONSCIOUS ACTION
MORNING ROUTINE	Wake up, scroll phone	No - Disconnected	Start with breath and silence
WORKDAY	Reactive emails	No - Out of Alignment	Block time for deep focus
FOOD	Irregular schedule	No - Disembodied	Schedule nourishing breaks

Reflection Prompt:

Where in my life am I living out of memory, not intention?

Conscious Practices That Anchor Remembering

1. Intentional Mornings – How we start the day creates a cognitive frame (Goleman, 2013)

2. Breath Awareness – Consciously guiding breath reduces amygdala reactivity and increases prefrontal regulation (Zeidan et al., 2010)

3. Movement – Physical activity increases BDNF (brain-derived neurotrophic factor), essential for emotional and cognitive flexibility

4. Mindful Eating – Reconnects us to the body, anchoring awareness in the present moment

5. Precious Pauses – Micro-moments of stillness recalibrate the nervous system

Commitment Practice: Conscious Anchoring

Each day this week, choose 3 conscious anchors:

- Morning Anchor: 5 minutes of breath before checking phone
- Midday Anchor: Eat one meal in silence
- Evening Anchor: Reflect on one action that honored your truth

Journal Prompt:

What changed in my sense of self when I honored these anchors?

The Risk of Skipping the Surface

Too often, seekers want to go deep immediately.

But if we neglect the conscious layer, we fall into:

- Spiritual bypassing
- Emotional flooding
- Cognitive dissonance
- Burnout

We must build the vessel before we pour in the Precious.

That vessel is your conscious structure.

Integration Table		
CONSCIOUS ACTION	**WHAT IT SUPPORTS**	**REMEMBERING IMPACT**
International breath	Nervous system regulation	Creates space for awareness
Body movement	Emotional discharge	Restores energy and clarity
Structured day	Cognitive order	Reduces overwhelm and distraction
Stilness pauses	Reflection time	Invites inner voice forward
Healthy food	Gut-brain axis support	Stabilizes mood and focus

In Summary

The conscious layer is not a detour.

It is the doorway.

It's where remembering begins:

With the breath.

The choice.

The pattern.

The practice.

The Precious is not somewhere else.

It's in how you show up today.

Right here.

Right now.

One action at a time.

References

- Doidge, N. (2007). The brain that changes itself: Stories of personal triumph from the frontiers of brain science.

- Kays, J. L., Hurley, R. A., & Taber, K. H. (2012). The dynamic brain: Neuroplasticity and mental health. The Journal of Neuropsychiatry and Clinical Neurosciences, 24(2), 118–124.

- Zeidan, F., Johnson, S. K., Diamond, B. J., et al. (2010). Mindfulness meditation improves cognition: Evidence of brief mental training. Consciousness and Cognition, 19(2), 597–605.

- Goleman, D. (2013). Focus: The hidden driver of excellence.

Chapter 5: Preconscious Remembering

The Patterns That Live Just Beneath the Surface

Until you make the unconscious conscious, it will direct your life and you will call it fate.

— Carl Jung

But before we reach the unconscious,

we must pass through the veil of the preconscious—

that subtle, slippery in-between where stories are formed,

scripts are rehearsed,

and identities take shape.

This is the place where memory lives—

but slightly out of reach.

The story we live…

without realizing we're repeating it.

The Dialogue

Clinician: You say you keep ending up in the same kind of relationship.

Patient: Yes, it's like I know it's not good for me—but I go back anyway.

Clinician: Do you remember the first time it felt familiar?

Patient: (pause) Actually… yes. It's like I'm trying to fix something I couldn't fix as a kid.

Clinician: That's the preconscious talking. It remembers—even if you don't.

Understanding the Preconscious Layer

The preconscious is the bridge:

- Not fully in awareness like the conscious
- Not deeply buried like the unconscious
- But close enough to surface—if we listen

It holds:

- Core beliefs
- Schema
- Long-held emotions
- Early impressions
- Conditioned roles and internalized voices

These are not repressed, but habitual.

They run silently—until something brings them to light.

Scientific Insight

Schemas are internalized mental frameworks formed early in life.

According to Schema Therapy, these shape how we interpret relationships, threats, and self-worth (Young et al., 2003). When activated, they drive automatic thoughts, emotions, and behaviors—without our conscious awareness.

Example Schemas:

- Defectiveness/Shame: I'm not lovable.
- Abandonment: People will always leave me.
- Unrelenting Standards: I must be perfect to be accepted.

Tool: Schema Reflection Map

The Schema Reflection Map is designed to help individuals surface and explore the preconscious schemas that influence their thoughts, emotions, behaviors, and interpersonal patterns. This tool brings implicit beliefs closer to conscious awareness, allowing for examination and transformation through reflection and intentional re-mapping.

Step 1: Identify the Trigger

Recall a recent situation where you felt emotionally reactive or unsettled. Briefly describe the event below:

- Triggering Situation:

Step 2: Surface the Schema

Reflect on what underlying belief or story might have been activated. Common schemas include abandonment, unworthiness, failure, mistrust, emotional deprivation, etc.

- What belief was triggered?

Step 3: Trace Its Origin

When do you first remember feeling this way? Who or what contributed to its formation?

- Early memory or pattern origin:

Step 4: Identify Behavioral Patterns

How do you typically respond when this schema is activated? What's the behavioral pattern?

- Usual response pattern:

Step 5: Challenge and Reframe

What evidence do you have that challenges this schema? What would a more accurate or empowering belief be?

- Reframed belief or alternative narrative:

Step 6: Commit to a New Response

What conscious behavior can you practice next time this schema is activated?

- New commitment:

Final Reflection

What did you learn about yourself through this reflection? How does this process help you reclaim your preconscious mind as a source of healing?

TRIGGERING SITUATION	Emotional Response	Automatic Thought	Underlying Belief (Schema)	New Conscious Statement
CRITICIZED AT WORK	Shame	I'm not good enough	Defectiveness	I am learning, not failing
PARTNER CANCELS PLANS	Anxiety	They're pulling away	Abandonment	I am safe. I am whole.

Reflection Prompt:

What's the oldest memory that echoes this feeling?

Preconscious Patterns and Relationships

Much of our suffering comes not from new wounds —

but from old ones relived in new forms.

We don't see people as they are.
We see them as someone else.
And we play out a part we never got to finish.

— **Mardoche Sidor, MD**

Modality Integration:

- Attachment theory: Our early attachment styles form preconscious relational blueprints (Ainsworth, Bowlby)
- ACT: Defusion practices help us observe beliefs without fusing with them
- Gestalt: Empty chair work gives voice to internalized others
- Mindfulness: Helps us witness thoughts and emotions as events—not truths

Practice: The Origin Script Exercise

1. Identify a recurring emotional trigger (rejection, failure)
2. Ask: When did I first feel this way?
3. Ask again: Who was there? What did I need? What did I learn?
4. Now rewrite: What do I choose to believe today?

This is the work of re-authoring the self.

The Role of Memory in Preconscious Healing

Memory stored in the preconscious is often symbolic, not narrative.

You may remember a smell, a song, a glance—a feeling that makes no sense until traced back.

The body remembers what the mind forgets.

— Bessel van der Kolk

This is why healing often begins with recognition before understanding.

Integration Table

Level	Process	Key Insight	Practice
Conscious	New actions	I am what I do repeatedly	Anchoring routines
Preconscious	Schema awareness	I carry old beliefs into new places	Schema Reflection Map
Unconscious	Deep release	I buried pain to protect myself	Free association, dreamwork

Commitment Practice: Pattern Tracking

For the next 7 days, track one recurring emotional response.

At the end of each day, write:

- What triggered it?
- What belief came up?
- What memory might it be linked to?
- What new truth can I choose now?

This is how we move from living in repetition to living in remembrance.

In Summary

The preconscious is a powerful guide.

It doesn't shout.

But it repeats.

If we listen closely, we'll hear its voice:

Not as judgment.

But as invitation.

To return to the place where the pattern was born—

And to choose, this time,

not to repeat…

but to remember.

References

- Young, J. E., Klosko, J. S., & Weishaar, M. E. (2003). Schema Therapy: A Practitioner's Guide.

- Bowlby, J. (1988). A Secure Base: Parent-Child Attachment and Healthy Human Development.

- van der Kolk, B. (2014). The Body Keeps the Score.

- Hayes, S. C., Strosahl, K. D., & Wilson, K. G. (1999). Acceptance and Commitment Therapy.

- Perls, F., Hefferline, R., & Goodman, P. (1951). Gestalt Therapy: Excitement and Growth in the Human Personality.

Chapter 6: Unconscious Remembering

Where the Deepest Wounds—and the Deepest
Wisdom—Reside

There is no coming to consciousness without pain.

— **Carl Jung**

We are now entering the deepest layer.

Where the stories we couldn't bear to feel got stored.

Where memory lost its words

and became sensation, symptom, silence.

This is the unconscious.

Where the forgotten goes to sleep—

not to disappear,

but to wait.

The Dialogue

Clinician: You said you don't know why you react so strongly to being ignored.

Patient: Yes. It's like I go numb. Or explode. I don't understand it.

Clinician: Might you be wondering whether that might be because the part of you reacting isn't the adult you.

Patient: Then who is it?

Clinician: Wondering whether that might be the part that never got to speak. The one who learned it wasn't safe to feel.

Patient: (becomes tearful) But I don't remember that part.

Clinician: Not yet. But it remembers you.

Understanding the Unconscious Layer

The unconscious is not just below awareness.

It's defended against awareness.

Here lives:

- Repressed memories
- Primitive fears
- Symbolic dreams
- Forgotten griefs
- Early trauma
- Unprocessed sensations

The unconscious shapes how we see the world—without us ever knowing it.

Scientific Insight

Repression is the brain's protective mechanism to prevent overwhelming material from flooding conscious awareness. But repressed material doesn't disappear—it reappears:

- In symptoms
- In dreams
- In projections
- In reenactments

Neuroscience confirms that trauma and early relational experiences are stored in nonverbal memory systems, such as the amygdala, hippocampus, and insular cortex (Schore, 2003; van der Kolk, 2014).

Tool: Free Association Practice

Sit with pen and paper.

Write one word (fear, abandon, mother).

Then without editing, let your hand move.

Don't think—follow the thread.

When emotion arises, pause.

Breathe.

Then write again.

This is the language of the unconscious:

irrational, nonlinear, yet utterly truthful.

Working Through: The Three Phases of Unconscious Integration

- Reconnection – through free association, dreams, bodily awareness

- Reprocessing – using safe relational containers to name and hold

- Integration – creating new meaning, insight, and narrative

Modality Integration:

- Psychoanalysis: Free association, dreamwork, transference

- Somatic Experiencing: Tracking body sensations to release trapped trauma

- EMDR: Bilateral stimulation to unlock stuck trauma memories

- Internal Family Systems (IFS): Accessing exiled parts of the psyche

Practice: Dream Inquiry

Each morning, write your dreams.

Even fragments.

Then ask:

- What is the feeling tone?

- What part of me might this represent?

- What is the dream asking me to feel or remember?

Integration Table

Level	Process	Key Insight	Practice
Conscious	Behavior	Alarm Clock	Anchored habits
Preconscious	Core belief	Repeated emotional trigger	Schema Reflection Map
Unconscious	Deep symbolic memory	Dream, slip, projection	Free Association, Dream Log

Commitment Practice: Unconscious Companioning

Choose one moment this week where you overreacted.

Instead of judging yourself, sit and ask:

- Who in me reacted?

- When did I first feel this way?

- What wasn't safe to feel then, that I can feel now?

Then place your hand on your heart.

Whisper: I see you. I remember you. You are safe now.

In Summary

To remember unconsciously is not to recall facts.

It is to feel again.

To honor the pain we once had to exile.

To welcome back the parts of us we had to abandon in order to survive.

And in doing so—

we become whole.

References

- van der Kolk, B. A. (2014). The Body Keeps the Score.
- Schore, A. N. (2003). Affect Dysregulation and Disorders of the Self.
- Freud, S. (1915). The Unconscious.
- Jung, C. G. (1964). Man and His Symbols.
- Gendlin, E. T. (1982). Focusing.
- Ogden, P., Minton, K., & Pain, C. (2006). Trauma and the Body.

Chapter 7: Existential Remembering

Identity, Meaning, and the Precious Question:
Who Am I?

You do not have to become yourself. You only need to remember.

Opening Scene – A Dialogue

Patient: I've done the work. The therapy. The journaling. I've changed habits, I've healed patterns. But something still feels... off. Like I'm living someone else's life.

Clinician: What if the next layer isn't about what you fix—but what you uncover?

Patient: Uncover?

Clinician: Yes. The self beneath all of this—the part of you that was never broken. The part that remembers.

Scientific Insight

Neuroscience shows that our sense of identity is not static, but constructed over time in relationship to our memories, environment, and core beliefs. According to narrative identity research (McAdams, 2001), it is not the events of our lives that determine well-being, but the meaning we make of them.

When trauma occurs, the brain suppresses or fragments parts of our identity to protect us. This is often associated with altered activity in the default mode network, the neural network involved in self-referential processing (Northoff et al., 2006).

Existential psychotherapy (Yalom, 1980) teaches us that many symptoms we treat as pathology are, in fact, the result of disconnection—from meaning, from values, and from a sense of self-authorship. Healing, at this level, is not about symptom reduction. It's about identity restoration.

The Tool – The Remembered Self Inquiry

This exercise helps individuals reconnect with identity beyond roles, trauma, or external conditioning.

Step 1: Strip the Roles

Begin by naming and releasing false identifiers. Say aloud:

- I am not my job.
- I am not my trauma.
- I am not my role.
- I am not my story.

Pause after each. Notice what remains.

Step 2: Ask the Precious Questions

- Who was I before I had to protect myself?
- What does my soul long for?
- What part of me has always been present—even when I forgot?

Write down or speak what arises without judgment.

Step 3: Listen with the Body

- Sit in stillness for two minutes.
- Breathe into the heart, belly, and throat.
- Ask: Who am I beneath everything I've performed?
- Let the body respond—through sensation, image, word, or stillness.

Optional Practice

Stand in front of a mirror. Look softly at yourself and say:

I remember who I am.

Repeat three times. Breathe deeply.

Clinical Integration

Existential remembering emerges once clients have stabilized at the behavioral (conscious) level, gained emotional insight (pre-conscious), and begun to process repressed content (unconscious).

Use this layer of work when:

- The client expresses chronic disconnection or lack of meaning
- Insight is present but lacks integration
- Identity is fluid or confusing (I don't know who I am anymore)

In session:

- Invite value exploration and life visioning
- Use narrative techniques to construct I am statements grounded in essence
- Reflect on clients' shifts in tone, language, and internal authority

Key Indicators of Existential Integration:

- Increased calm and congruence
- Decisions rooted in values, not fear
- Boundaries set without overexplaining
- Sense of presence in speech, posture, and energy

Reflection Prompt

When I stop trying to be who I think I should be… what remains?

Write this at the top of your journal page. Answer without editing. Read it back. Then place one hand on your heart and whisper:

This is who I am. I remember now.

Closing Words from the Soul

You never needed to become anything.

You only needed to allow what was already true to speak again.

And it is speaking.

Beneath the noise. Beneath the shame.

It is saying,

'I've been here all along.'

Suggested Practice for the Week

Each day, take five quiet minutes to ask yourself:

What part of me is present right now?

Note the answer—without judgment.

Breathe into that part.

Give it thanks.

Let it remind you:

You never left.

You only forgot.

References

- McAdams, D. P. (2001). The Psychology of Life Stories. Review of General Psychology, 5(2), 100–122. https://doi.org/10.1037/1089-2680.5.2.100

- Northoff, G., Heinzel, A., de Greck, M., Bermpohl, F., Dobrowolny, H., & Panksepp, J. (2006). Self-referential processing in our brain—a meta-analysis of imaging studies on the self. NeuroImage, 31(1), 440–457. https://doi.org/10.1016/j.neuroimage.2005.12.002

- Yalom, I. D. (1980). Existential Psychotherapy. Basic Books.

- Singer, J. A., & Blagov, P. (2004). Self-defining memories, narrative identity, and psychotherapy: A conceptual model to guide empirical research. In D. Beike, J. Lampinen, & D. Behrend (Eds.), The Self and Memory (pp. 117–138). Psychology Press.

- Frankl, V. E. (2006). Man's Search for Meaning. Beacon Press. (Original work published 1946)

Chapter 8: Integration

Weaving the layers into Wholeness

We are not fragmented beings trying to become whole. We are whole beings learning to remember.

— Karen Dubin, PhD, LCSW

We began at the surface.

We moved through the patterns.

We reached into the depths.

And now, we integrate.

Because insight is not enough.

Action is not enough.

Even remembering is not enough—

until it changes us.

True transformation doesn't happen in a flash.

It happens in a spiral—

Revisiting the same wounds,

but from higher ground.

The Dialogue

Patient: I had a breakthrough last week. I remembered something huge.

Clinician: That's powerful. Tell me what you did with that remembering.

Patient: (pause) I don't know… it felt important. But I didn't change anything.

Clinician: So you seem to be saying that the memory hasn't become integrated yet. It's still living alone.

Patient: So what do I do?

Clinician: How do you feeling about bringing it to all three levels. Giving it breath. Giving it structure. Giving it voice?

Why Integration Matters

Remembering without integration can leave us flooded, paralyzed, or self-critical.

Action without insight can lead to burnout.

Insight without action can create guilt.

We must weave all three levels—

Not in order once, but over and over again.

The Topographical Integration Spiral

The Topographical Integration Spiral is a therapeutic framework that helps clinicians and individuals integrate experiences, insights, and interventions across the three levels of the psyche—conscious, preconscious, and unconscious—using a spiral model of transformation. This framework illustrates that healing is not linear but occurs through repeated cycles of deeper integration, each time encompassing more complexity and awareness.

Overview of the Spiral

The spiral begins at the conscious level, moves through the preconscious, descends into the unconscious, and then rises back into the conscious mind. Each revolution through the spiral brings a greater depth of self-understanding and a higher level of wholeness. Unlike a linear path, the spiral allows for revisiting old material with new awareness.

Phases of the Spiral

1. Conscious Engagement

- Recognize present patterns, behaviors, and thoughts.
- Use tools like the Conscious Remembering Inventory.
- Explore what is known and already accessible to awareness.

2. Preconscious Exploration

- Identify underlying schemas, habitual narratives, and subtle emotional cues.
- Use mapping tools like the Schema Reflection Map to access this layer.
- Employ journaling, guided imagery, or projective techniques.

3. Unconscious Discovery

- Engage in deeper work such as dream analysis, shadow work, and memory reconsolidation.
- Use metaphor, storytelling, body memory awareness, and free association.
- Safe therapeutic environment is essential for this layer.

4. Integration & Re-Emergence

- Reflect, apply insight, and begin to live from a more whole, aware self.
- Use practices like active imagination, behavior shifts, and symbolic rituals.
- Recognize and honor the cycle: healing may revisit old material with new insight.

Clinical Application

Clinicians can use the Topographical Integration Spiral as a case formulation and treatment planning tool. It enables tailoring interventions to the client's current level of awareness and gradually deepening their work. It also helps avoid premature confrontation of unconscious material without sufficient ego strength.

Suggested Visualization

Imagine a spiral staircase with three major platforms: Conscious, Preconscious, and Unconscious. As the client climbs upward, they periodically circle back to familiar material, but from a new vantage point. The clinician can guide the ascent with clarity, compassion, and calibrated pacing.

Level	What it Holds	Transformation Happens Through
Conscious	Behavior, routine, structure	Anchoring and action
Preconscious	Beliefs, patterns, conditioned roles	Recognition and re-scripting
Unconscious	Repression, symbolic memory, trauma	Expression and integration

Scientific Insight: Tri-Level Learning

Behavioral science, neuroscience, and psychodynamic theory agree:

- Change that starts with behavior creates cognitive shifts (Kazdin, 2008)

- Change that restructures belief shifts emotional processing (Beck, 1979)

- Change that includes unconscious material prevents relapse and promotes wholeness (Freud, 1915; Jung, 1939)

Tool: Three-Level Integration Template

Three-Level Integration Template				
EXPERIENCE	CAUTIOUS ACTION	PRECONSCIOUS BELIEF	UNCONSCIOUS ORIGIN	WHAT INTEGRATION LOOKS LIKE
Avoiding success	I procrastinate	I'll be judged if I succeed.	Early memory of being shamed for standing out	I show up, even when scared. I hold both fear and worth.
People-pleasing	I say yes too much	If I say no, I'll be rejected.	Early neglect or conditional love	I honor my boundaries with compassion.

Practice Prompt:

Take any behavior or reaction this week. Ask:

- What am I doing? (Conscious)
- What belief is beneath this? (Preconscious)
- Where did I first learn that? (Unconscious)
- Then write a new integrated truth.

Reflection: The Spiral of Growth

You may feel like you're revisiting the same issue again.

That's not regression.

That's integration.

You are deeper now.

Wider now.

More spacious in how you hold yourself.

Healing isn't linear.

It spirals—until nothing is hidden, and everything belongs.

Commitment Practice: Weekly Spiral Reflection

Once a week, journal the following:

- What did I become aware of this week? (Conscious)
- What story or belief showed up again? (Preconscious)
- What old wound or image did I glimpse? (Unconscious)
- How can I act on this with love and clarity? (Integration)

You are not stuck.

You are spiraling home.

From Remembering to Becoming

Remembering is the bridge.

But becoming is the destination.

To remember is to reclaim every part of yourself:

The disciplined one.

The abandoned one.

The dreaming one.

The child.

The protector.

The guide.

And when all those parts speak with one voice—

That is integration.

That is peace.

References

- Freud, S. (1915). The Unconscious.

- Jung, C. G. (1939). The Integration of the Personality.

- Beck, A. T. (1979). Cognitive Therapy and the Emotional Disorders.

- Kazdin, A. E. (2008). Behavior Modification in Applied Settings.

- Siegel, D. J. (2012). The Developing Mind: How Relationships and the Brain Interact to Shape Who We Are.

Part III: The Science and the Soul

Chapter 9: Memory, the Brain, and the Mind

What Science Tells Us About How—and Why—We Remember

The past is not dead. It is not even past.
— William Faulkner

We like to believe memory is a file.

You open it, read it, close it.

Neat. Clear. Reliable.

But memory is more like mist.

It floats. It shifts.

It's rewritten each time we recall it.

And yet...

it shapes everything.

From who we trust,

to how we love,

to what we fear in the dark.

To remember is not just to access information—

It is to touch the architecture of the self.

The Dialogue

Patient: I can't remember much of my childhood. Just flashes. Emotions.

Clinician: Tell me the types of emotions?

Patient: Fear. Shame. But no clear scenes. Just... a feeling in my body.

Clinician: That's still memory. Just not the kind you were taught to look for.

TYPES OF MEMORY (AND WHY THEY MATTER)

MEMORY TYPE	DESCRIPTION	BRAIN REGION(S) INVOLVED	RELEVANCE TO REMEMBERING
EXPLICIT (DECLARATIVE)	Facts, events, autobiographical detail	Hippocampus, prefrontal cortex	I remember what happened.
IMPLICIT (NON-DECLARATIVE)	Habits, skills, conditioned responses	Basal ganglia, cerebellum	I don't remember, but I react.
EMOTIONAL	Fear, shame, love, stored as somatic cues	Amygdala, insula	I feel it in my body.
PROCEDURAL	Repetitive behavioral memory	Motor cortex, striatum	I keep doing this, without knowing why.

Key Insight:

The brain doesn't store memory like a video.

It stores fragments—sensory cues, emotions, meanings—scattered across different brain systems.

To remember is to reconstruct.

Scientific Insight

Memory is state-dependent—we are more likely to recall something when we are in the same emotional or physiological state in which it was formed (Eich, 1980).

This is why trauma survivors often cannot access the full story.

The memory lives in the body, not just in the mind.

Neuroscience confirms what therapy has long known, that the brain remembers everything—just not always in words.

— Karen Dubin, Ph.D., LCSW

The Hippocampus and the Amygdala: The Memory Gatekeepers

- Hippocampus – Organizes factual memory. It's like the brain's librarian.

- Amygdala – Tags emotional salience. If it's scary or powerful, the amygdala makes sure you don't forget— even if the details get blurred.

Trauma Tip:

High amygdala activation suppresses hippocampal functioning.

Meaning: the more intense the fear, the less clear the narrative.

This is why healing often begins with body-based remembering, not storytelling.

Tool: The Sensory Memory Map

When you feel triggered or unsettled, ask:

- What do I see, hear, smell, taste, or touch right now that feels familiar?

- Is there a time earlier in life when I felt the same way in my body?

- What might this moment be echoing from my past? (these are your emotional echoes)

Create a map of emotional echoes—not to analyze, but to track patterns over time. (do you have an example. What is meant here by a map. What does that look like)

Memory and Identity

Our memories form the scaffolding of identity.

- I am someone who was loved.
- I am someone who was left.
- I am someone who had to perform to be accepted.

But here's the secret:

Because memory is malleable, identity is malleable too.

Memory reconsolidation research (Lane et al., 2015) shows that when an emotional memory is reactivated and then reprocessed in a safe context, the brain can update the emotional meaning attached to it.

This is why therapy works.

This is why remembering in the presence of compassion changes everything.

Practice: Memory Re-authoring

Choose a vivid or recurring emotional memory.

Then ask:

- What did I believe about myself when this happened?
- What else might have been true that I didn't know then?
- What would I tell my younger self now?

Then write it as a new narrative:

Once upon a time, I believed… But now I know…

This is how remembering becomes liberating.

Integration Table

Level	How Memory Operates	Challenge	Path to Healing
Conscious	Recall, insight	Incomplete stories	Self-reflection, journaling
Preconscious	Repeated emotional patterns	Bias, distortions	Schema work, mindfulness
Unconscious	Symbol, body, dream	Regression, projection	Free association, somatic work

Commitment Practice: The Daily Remembering Prompt

Each evening, write:

- What did I remember today about who I am?

- What did my body tell me?

- What belief am I ready to update?

Over time, you'll begin to feel a shift—

Not just in memory, but in identity.

You are not becoming someone new.

You are recovering someone eternal.

In Summary

Memory is not just something you have.

It is something you live.

Something you carry.

Something you can reclaim.

To understand memory is to understand that you are not broken—you are layered.

And through awareness, compassion, and integration,you can become the author of your story again.

References

- Eich, E. (1980). The cue-dependent nature of state-dependent retrieval. Memory & Cognition, 8(2), 157–173.

- Lane, R. D., Ryan, L., Nadel, L., & Greenberg, L. (2015). Memory reconsolidation, emotional arousal, and the process of change in psychotherapy. Behavioral and Brain Sciences, 38, e31.

- Schore, A. N. (2003). Affect Dysregulation and Disorders of the Self.

- van der Kolk, B. A. (2014). The Body Keeps the Score.

- Phelps, E. A. (2006). Emotion and cognition: Insights from studies of the human amygdala. Annual Review of Psychology, 57, 27–53.

Chapter 10: Trauma and the Choice to Forget

When Forgetting Becomes Survival—and
Remembering Becomes Liberation

Trauma is not what happens to us.

***Trauma is what happens inside us as a result of what
happened.***

— Gabor Maté, MD

Forgetting is not weakness.

It is wisdom.

The body forgets because it had to.

The mind blocks because it was protecting.

And the soul…

waits.

It waits until we're strong enough

safe enough

whole enough

to remember

what once would have shattered us.

The Dialogue

Patient: There's so much I just don't remember.

Clinician: Tell me whether you blame yourself for that

Patient: Sometimes. It feels like something's wrong with me.

Clinician: What if forgetting was your brain's way of protecting
you?

Patient: Protecting me?

Clinician: Yes. Trauma teaches the mind to forget so the body can survive.

The Biology of Forgetting

When we experience trauma, the brain shifts into survival mode:

- The amygdala (alarm center) goes into overdrive.
- The hippocampus (memory organizer) shuts down.
- The prefrontal cortex (thinking and reasoning) goes offline.

In this state, memory becomes fragmented.

We remember sensations, not sequences.

Images, not explanations.

Reactions, not reasons.

This is not dysfunction.

It's design.

The brain does not distinguish between physical threat and emotional overwhelm.

In both cases, it prioritizes survival over coherence.

— Mardoche Sidor, MD

Scientific Insight

Trauma memory is stored as implicit memory—in the body and brain, but outside conscious awareness.

It is retrieved through triggers, dreams, emotional flashbacks, or even smells.

This explains why someone may:

- Panic in response to a tone of voice
- Dissociate when touched
- Cry during an ordinary conversation

Van der Kolk (2014) calls this the tyranny of the past.

But neuroscience also offers hope: through memory recon-solidation, the brain can re-edit traumatic memories under new emotional conditions.

Tool: The Trigger Reflection Template

This tool is designed to help you pause, reflect, and examine the deeper layers behind a triggering event. It invites exploration across conscious, preconscious, and unconscious levels to foster insight, integration, and healing.

Instructions:

Use this template whenever you feel triggered, unsettled, or emotionally activated. Complete it soon after the experience and review it later to track patterns and progress.

Trigger Reflection Template

- [ ] Describe the triggering event:

- [ ] What were your immediate thoughts or judgments?

- [ ] What emotions came up?

- [ ] What physical sensations did you notice?

- [ ] Conscious layer: What story or belief was activated?

- [ ] Preconscious layer: What memory or early pattern may this connect to?

- [ ] Unconscious layer: What fear, wound, or unmet need might be underneath?

- [ ] What did this moment invite you to remember about yourself?

- [ ] What might you choose to do or believe differently next time?

- [ ] Any closing insight or message for yourself?

TRIGGER MOMENT	PHYSICAL REACTION	EMOTION FELT	WHAT MIGHT THIS ECHO?	SAFETY STATEMENT
Someone raised voice	Tight chest	Fear	Dad yelling at dinner table	This is now. I am safe.

Practice Prompt:

Instead of asking, What's wrong with me?

Ask: What am I remembering without realizing it?

The Role of Dissociation

Dissociation is the nervous system's emergency escape hatch.

It numbs awareness.

Disconnects memory.

Preserves functioning.

But when overused, it fragments the self.

We forget who we are.

We lose continuity.

We feel like strangers inside our own skin.

Healing Dissociation Includes:

- Grounding practices (somatic and sensory)
- Relational safety (attachment repair)
- Gradual exposure to memory in manageable doses
- Integration across parts (e.g., in IFS or ego-state work)

Modality Integration

- **Somatic Experiencing (SE):** Helps release stored trauma via bodily awareness (Levine, 1997)
- **EMDR:** Desensitizes traumatic memories using bilateral stimulation (Shapiro, 2001)
- **IFS (Internal Family Systems):** Helps reconnect dissociated parts of the psyche (Schwartz, 2001)
- **Psychoanalysis:** Encourages gentle uncovering of repressed content through free association and dreamwork

Practice: The Safety Ladder (I don't get why this is called a ladder)

When traumatic memory arises, don't dive in—build a ladder.

1. Ground yourself in your body. (Breath, feet, senses.)
2. Remind yourself: I am safe. This memory is old.

3. Decide if now is the right time to go further—or if you need support.

4. Return when ready.

5. Journal what came up.

Integration is a choice. Pacing is power.

Integration Table

Level	Trauma's Impact	Healing Path	Primary Tools
Conscious	Avoidance, behavioral disruption	Grounded Structure	Routines, breath, nutrition
Preconscious	Distorted beliefs, hypervigilance	Cognitive restructuring	ACT, CBT, Schema Therapy
Unconscious	Repression, dissociation, flashbacks	Symbolic processing	SE, IFS, EMDR, Dreamwork

Commitment Practice: Remembering With Compassion

This week, commit to catching every moment of self-blame around forgetting, dissociating, or overreacting.

And instead say:

This was wisdom, not weakness. I remember slowly. I remember safely. I remember with grace.

In Summary

You didn't fail to remember.

You chose—on some deep, biological, soulful level—to protect yourself.

And now, as you grow,

as you build safety and structure,

as you reclaim your voice—

you are being invited

not to relive the pain,

but to remember the strength

that got you here.

This is not a return to the trauma.

It is a return to you.

References

- van der Kolk, B. A. (2014). The Body Keeps the Score.
- Schore, A. N. (2003). Affect Dysregulation and the Origin of the Self.
- Levine, P. A. (1997). Waking the Tiger: Healing Trauma.
- Shapiro, F. (2001). Eye Movement Desensitization and Reprocessing (EMDR).
- Schwartz, R. C. (2001). Internal Family Systems Therapy.
- Lane, R. D. et al. (2015). Memory reconsolidation, emotional arousal, and the process of change in psychotherapy. Behavioral and Brain Sciences.

Chapter 11: The Developmental Roots of Who We Are

How Early Experiences Shape the Self—and How We Begin Again

Tell me how you were loved, and I'll tell you how you live.
— Karen Dubin, Ph.D., LCSW

Before we had language,

we had sensation.

Before we had memory,

we had relationship.

And from relationship—

we formed identity.

We learned who we were

by how we were held.

Spoken to.

Fed.

Seen.

Ignored.

Responded to—or not.

And so, much of what we call personality...

is really adaptation.

The Dialogue

Clinician: You describe yourself as 'too much.' Tell me where that came from.

Patient: I've always been intense. Emotional. I guess I just am that way.

Clinician: Oh... Tell me if someone once treated your feelings as too much.

Patient: (pause) Yes. My mom. She used to tell me I was exhausting.

Clinician: And so the part of you that felt fully alive learned to hide.

Patient: (quietly) I thought it was just who I am. But maybe it's who I became.

The Architecture of the Self

From birth through early childhood, we are developing:

- Attachment templates
- Emotional regulation patterns
- Core beliefs about self and others
- Relational scripts
- Implicit memory structures

These become our internal working models—the mental blueprints that guide:

- How safe we feel in the world
- What we expect from others
- How we treat ourselves

If we were ignored, we learn to shrink.

If we were criticized, we learn to strive.

If we were adored for performance, we learn to disappear when we rest.

Scientific Insight: Attachment and Brain Wiring

Secure attachment in early life predicts:

- Greater emotion regulation capacity (Schore, 2001)
- Stronger executive functioning (prefrontal cortex)
- Lower amygdala reactivity to stress
- Higher resilience and empathy later in life (Siegel, 2012)

Conversely, neglect, misattunement, or chaos led to overactivation of survival circuits and impaired development of self-regulation systems.

This means:

You didn't become anxious for no reason.

You were shaped by thousands of micro-moments.

Tool: The Developmental Timeline Map

Draw a timeline from birth to age 18.

Then note:

- Moments of felt safety
- Moments of emotional rupture or neglect
- Core messages you internalized at each stage

AGE	SIGNIFICANT EVENT	FEELING	INTERNALIZED BELIEF	ADAPTATION
4	Mom left for work crying	Confused, sad	I'm too much when I need love	Became self-reliant
10	Praised only when achieving	Proud, but pressure	I must perform to be valued	Overachiever, perfectionist

Reflection Prompt:

Whose love did I adapt myself to receive?

The Concept of Symbolic Memory

Not all early experience is remembered with words.

In fact, the earliest years of life are stored symbolically—in the body, in images, in emotion.

This is called preverbal or implicit memory.

> *The infant has no words—but absorbs the world like a sponge.*
> *And from that soaking, meaning is made.*
> *— Mardoche Sidor, MD*

This is why someone may feel:

- Deep fear in intimacy
- Guilt when resting
- Unexplainable sadness in moments of joy

Not because of now—

but because of then.

Modality Integration

- **Attachment-Based Therapy**: Repairs early ruptures through safe relational mirroring

- **Inner Child Work**: Reconnects with the unmet needs of early self-states

- **Sensorimotor Psychotherapy**: Uses the body to access preverbal memory

- **Narrative Therapy**: Helps reclaim the story by tracing it back to origin

Practice: Inner Reparenting Ritual

Each morning this week:

1. Sit quietly. Place your hand on your heart.

2. Imagine your 3-year-old self in front of you.

3. Say aloud:

   - You are not too much. Vs You are enough – I thought there was no not in the unconscious

   - You are safe now.

   - You are allowed to rest.

   - I love you, exactly as you are.

This rewires symbolic memory with new emotional truth.

INTEGRATION TABLE

DEVELOPMENTAL INFLUENCE	BELIEF FORMED	ADULT ADAPTATION	HEALING DIRECTION
IGNORED WHEN SAD	My feelings are a burden	Emotional suppression	Relearning emotional expression
PRAISED FOR GRADES ONLY	I must earn love	Overworking	Reclaiming intrinsic worth
PARENT ABANDONED FAMILY	People leave	Fear of intimacy	Building secure internal attachment

Commitment Practice: This Is Me Map

The 'This Is Me Map' is a tool for self-discovery and integration, designed to help you explore the layers of your identity through the lens of conscious, preconscious, unconscious, and existential remembering. Use this tool to reflect, map, and navigate your journey back to your whole self.

Instructions

1. Print or draw a large circle on a blank page. Divide the circle into four quadrants.

2. Label each quadrant with one of the following: Conscious, Preconscious, Unconscious, Existential.

3. Use the guiding questions below to fill in each section of your map.

4. After completing your map, review what patterns emerge. What themes repeat across quadrants? Where do you feel most remembered, and where do you feel most disconnected?

5. Use this map as a living document—update it as you continue your process.

Quadrant Reflection Prompts

Conscious Layer

- What do I do regularly that reflects who I believe I am?
- What roles do I play daily (e.g., parent, clinician, friend)?
- What are my current values and priorities?

Preconscious Layer

- What patterns or habits do I repeat without much thought?
- What beliefs or assumptions influence my decisions?
- What emotional responses feel familiar but automatic?

Unconscious Layer

- What fears or wounds may be influencing me behind the scenes?
- What defense mechanisms or internalized messages still linger?
- What dreams, slips, or projections offer insight into this layer?

Existential Layer

- What gives my life meaning?
- Who am I, beneath my name, history, and personality?
- What do I sense my soul is here to express or experience?

Remember: This map is not about perfection or certainty. It's a mirror, a compass, and a doorway back to your true self. Let it evolve with you.

Who I Became	Who I Am Remembering
Always productive	Still worthy when I rest
Pleasing everyone	Honoring my own truth
Always strong	Allowed to feel and be held

Do this each week. Watch it change. Watch you change.

In Summary

Your past is not your prison.

It is your pattern.

And patterns can be softened.

Rewritten.

Reclaimed.

You are not your wounds.

You are the one who lived through them.

And now—

you are the one remembering.

References

- Schore, A. N. (2001). The effects of early relational trauma on right brain development, affect regulation, and infant mental health. Infant Mental Health Journal, 22(1–2), 201–269.

- Siegel, D. J. (2012). The Developing Mind.

- Bowlby, J. (1988). A Secure Base.

- Van der Kolk, B. A. (2014). The Body Keeps the Score.

- Porges, S. W. (2011). The Polyvagal Theory.

Chapter 12: Before This Life – Ancient Memory and Precious Contracts

Did I Choose This Life? And If So, Why?

You are not a human being having a spiritual experience.
You are a spiritual being having a human experience.

— Pierre Teilhard de Chardin

We've explored the conscious.

We've unearthed the preconscious.

We've remembered the unconscious.

But what if…

There is memory before memory?

What if forgetting didn't begin in childhood —

but in the womb?

Or before the womb?

What if some part of us knew,

before the body,

before the name,

before the story —

and chose?

The Dialogue

Patient: I keep asking, 'Why me?' Why this life? These parents? This pain?

Clinician: It's a powerful question. What if it's not random?

Patient: You think I chose this?

Clinician: Let's entertain the possibility—not to blame, but to empower.

Patient: (quietly) If I chose it...maybe I'm not a victim.

Clinician: Tell me if you think that perhaps you might be a soul in process, remembering its path.

Precious Contracts: A Metaphysical Framework

Psychologist Carolyn Myss coined the phrase Sacred Contracts—the idea that the soul agrees to certain lessons, relationships, and challenges before rebirth.

In this view, suffering isn't punishment.

It's curriculum.

What if that difficult parent...

was your soul's invitation to learn boundaries?

What if the chronic illness...

was an entry point into compassion?

What if the loss...

was a portal to remembering eternity?

Scientific Resonance: Quantum and Cellular Memory

While science doesn't yet fully prove pre-birth memory, compelling adjacent findings include:

- **Epigenetics**: Trauma and resilience can be passed down across generations (Yehuda et al., 2005)

- **Cellular memory**: Some transplant recipients report new preferences or memories (Pearsall et al., 1999)

- **Near-death experiences (NDEs):** Thousands describe awareness beyond brain activity (van Lommel, 2001)

- **Children's past-life recall**: Documented in multiple cultures with verified details (Stevenson, 2001)

> *Science is catching up to the soul.*
>
> — **Karen Dubin, Ph.D., LCSW**

Tool: The Precious inquiry Journal

This journal is designed to accompany Chapter 12: 'When We Remember, Everything Changes.' It invites you to reflect deeply on your core values, sacred experiences, and moments of insight that have marked your path. Use it to cultivate awe, gratitude, and clarity as you transition from survival to sacred living.

How to Use This Journal

You may complete one prompt each day, one per week, or allow yourself to return to specific prompts intuitively. Use this space freely—write poetry, draw, bullet journal, or simply note a single word. Let the inquiry be personal, spacious, and sacred.

Inquiry Prompts

1. What do I find precious about being alive today?
2. When have I felt most connected to something greater than myself?
3. What memory makes me feel full of light?
4. What have I forgotten that I now wish to remember?
5. What within me feels sacred and true?
6. Who or what has helped me remember who I really am?
7. What is a gift I am carrying that I haven't fully shared yet?
8. What am I afraid to remember—and what might be waiting behind that fear?
9. What would I do if I truly knew I was loved, guided, and whole?
10. What does sacred living look like for me?

Reflection Space

Use the table that follow for your reflections. You may duplicate it as needed. There is no right or wrong way to engage with this journal—only the invitation to show up, honestly and gently.

Inquiry Prompt	Reflection
If I chose this family, what was I meant to learn?	
If I chose this wound, what strength might it awaken?	
What patterns feel older than this life?	
What gifts have come from my greatest pain?	

Note: This is not a tool for spiritual bypassing.

We don't blame people for their trauma.

We offer them a lens of agency over meaning.

Modality Integration

- **Logotherapy (Frankl):** Healing through meaning

- **Jungian Depth Psychology:** Embraces the archetypal and collective unconscious

- **Transpersonal Therapy:** Integrates spiritual identity and cosmic consciousness

- **Narrative Therapy:** Allows for re-authoring and soul-centered reframing

When we rewrite our story through the lens of the soul, we stop asking 'Why me?' and begin asking, 'What now?'

Practice: The Remembering Meditation

Each morning, try this:

1. Sit with eyes closed.

2. Place both hands on your heart.

3. Say aloud or inwardly:

    a. I am not lost. I am remembering.

    b. There is a deeper purpose unfolding.

    c. I chose love. I choose it again.

4. Imagine yourself before this life—calm, wise, choosing this life for growth.

5. Then open your eyes and live as though you meant to be here.

INTEGRATION TABLE

FRAMEWORK	CORE QUESTION	EMPOWERING FRAME	PRACTICE
PRECIOUS CONTRACT	Why was this path chosen?	I chose to grow, even through pain	Precious inquiry Journal
ARCHETYPE	What is my mythic identity?	I am more than my wounds	Reflective storytelling
PATTERN MEMORY	What keeps repeating?	This is my opportunity to transform it	Spiral Reflection Practice

Commitment Practice: My Soul's Note

Tonight, write a letter from your soul to your human self.

Begin with:

Dear one,

Before you arrived in this body, you and I made a promise...

Then let the letter flow.

Let it remind you of who you are.

And why you're here.

Read it aloud when you forget.

In Summary

Maybe you didn't come here to succeed.

Maybe you came to remember.

To return to the truth that cannot be lost.

To live from the soul.

To walk through this life as one who chose.

And if that's true—

then even your forgetting was precious.

And your remembering…

is liberation.

References

- Myss, C. (2001). Precious Contracts: Awakening Your Divine Potential.

- Yehuda, R. et al. (2005). Transgenerational effects of trauma: Epigenetic mechanisms.

- Pearsall, P., Schwartz, G. E., & Russek, L. G. (1999). Changes in heart transplant recipients that parallel the personalities of their donors.

- van Lommel, P. (2001). Near-death experience in survivors of cardiac arrest. The Lancet, 358(9298), 2039–2045.

- Stevenson, I. (2001). Children Who Remember Previous Lives: A Question of Reincarnation.

- Frankl, V. E. (1959). Man's Search for Meaning.

Part IV: The Return

Chapter 13: When We Remember, Everything Changes

The Shift from Survival to Precious Living

The moment you remember who you are, the world no longer has power over you.

— Mardoche Sidor, MD

It happens subtly.

You stop blaming.

You stop chasing.

You stop waiting for permission to live.

And you start breathing differently.

Walking differently.

Listening more deeply.

This is what happens when you remember.

The Dialogue

Patient: It's strange. I still have the same job, same body, same circumstances… but everything feels different.

Clinician: Tell me what's changed.

Patient: (smiles softly) I remembered it's not about proving anything. I remembered I'm already enough.

Clinician: And tell me how that changes your choices.

Patient: I don't react the same way anymore. I respond. I don't need to escape. I just… am.

Clinician: That's it. That's the shift. From forgetting to presence. From identity to essence.

The Anatomy of a Shift

True transformation is not loud.

It doesn't arrive with fireworks.

It arrives with peace.

Because when we remember…

- We no longer need constant validation
- We let go of compulsive doing
- We become available to the present
- We align with flow instead of forcing outcomes

This is the neuroscience of integration:

- Prefrontal cortex (awareness, choice)
- Anterior cingulate cortex (empathy, regulation)
- Default mode network deactivation (ego quieting)
- Parasympathetic activation (rest-and-restore)

In other words:

When we remember, the brain rebalances. The body exhales. The self stabilizes.

Tool: The Shift Awareness Tracker

This tool is designed to help individuals become aware of the subtle and profound shifts that occur when they begin to remember who they truly are. Use this tracker to document moments of alignment, disconnection, and restoration as you move from survival mode to sacred living.

Instructions

Use this tracker daily or weekly. Note the situations in which you noticed a shift in your thoughts, emotions, behaviors, or sense of identity. Describe the situation, the shift you experienced, what triggered it, and how you responded or integrated the shift.

Shift Awareness Tracker Table				
DATE	SITUATION/CONTEXT	SHIFT OBSERVED	TRIGGER/CUE	RESPONSE/ INTEGRATION

Reflection Prompts

- What types of situations most commonly lead to helpful shifts?

- What patterns do you notice in how you respond to those shifts?

- What supports your ability to stay aligned with your true self?

MOMENT	OLD REACTION	NEW RESPONSE	WHAT HELPED ME REMEMBER
CRITICISM AT WORK	Defensiveness	Calm explanation	Breath. Grounding. I'm not defined by this.
FEELING LEFT OUT	Withdraw, overthink	Reach out and share	Recalled my pattern and shifted it
MORNING STRESS	Rush, tension	Gentle slowness	Precious Pause Practice

Practice Prompt:

Today, where did I pause instead of react?

What reminded me of who I am?

Living in Alignment

Remembering brings us back into alignment with:

- Purpose
- Presence
- Peace
- Power—not domination, but inner congruence

This is the end of self-abandonment.

The end of performing for love.

The beginning of living from love.

Modality Integration: The Embodied Shift

- ACT (Acceptance and Commitment Therapy): Teaches us to live by values, not fear
- **IFS (Internal Family Systems):** Restores leadership of the Self over exiled parts
- **Neuroscience of flow states:** Shows us the brain operates optimally when relaxed and engaged (Csikszentmihalyi, 1990)
- **Polyvagal Theory:** Reminds us that safety is the foundation of connection, creativity, and consciousness

Practice: Live As If Exercise

Choose one remembered truth—something you've reclaimed about yourself.

Then for 24 hours, live as if it were already fully embodied.

Examples:

- I am safe. → Take a risk you've avoided
- I am worthy. → Speak up in the meeting
- I am not broken. → Stop over-apologizing
- I belong here. → Walk with your head up

Notice:

- What shifts?
- What challenges emerge?
- What grows stronger in you?

This is remembering in motion.

Integration Table

REMEMBERED TRUTH	OLD PATTERN	NEW PATTERN	DAILY ANCHOR
I AM WHOLE	Seeking Constant Approval	Trusting Self in Silence	Morning Mirror Mantra
I AM GUIDED	Overplanning	Letting Go and Listening	Breath Before Decisions
I AM ENOUGH	Overworking	Rest Without Guilt	Scheduled Precious Pause

Commitment Practice: The Precious Mirror

Each morning, stand before a mirror.

Look yourself in the eyes.

Say aloud:

- I remember who I am.
- I don't need to become—only to be.
- I walk in alignment with truth, today.

Repeat for 21 days.

Watch what shifts.

In Summary

When we forget, we strive.

When we remember, we flow.

When we forget, we suffer.

When we remember, we serve.

When we forget, we try to become.

When we remember, we return to what always was.

This is not the end of your healing.

It is the beginning of your wholeness.

References

- Csikszentmihalyi, M. (1990). Flow: The Psychology of Optimal Experience.
- Porges, S. W. (2011). The Polyvagal Theory.
- Hayes, S. C., Strosahl, K. D., & Wilson, K. G. (1999). Acceptance and Commitment Therapy.
- Schwartz, R. C. (2001). Internal Family Systems Therapy.
- Siegel, D. J. (2012). The Developing Mind.

Chapter 14: The World Becomes Friendly Again

Reclaiming Trust, Flow, and Belonging

The most important decision we make is whether we believe we live in a friendly or hostile universe.

— Albert Einstein

When we forget who we are,

the world feels threatening.

Every silence feels like rejection.

Every uncertainty feels like danger.

Every mistake feels like proof that we're unworthy.

But when we remember—

everything softens.

The same world,

but through new eyes.

Eyes that no longer look for threat.

Eyes that remember:

I am not separate. I am home.

The Dialogue

Patient: Things still happen—stress, conflict, bad news. But I don't spiral anymore.

Clinician: Tell me what you do instead.

Patient: I breathe. I stay. I ask what it's here to teach me.

Clinician: That's trust.

Patient: It's strange, but... I feel like the world is on my side now.

Clinician: What if it always was. What if you just couldn't see it through fear?

Fear Makes the World Hostile

When we live from fear, our nervous system is primed for:

- Hypervigilance
- Misinterpretation
- Projection
- Control
- Avoidance

Fear filters every interaction through a survival lens:

Are they against me?

Am I safe here?

What if I fail?

What if I'm not enough?

And so the world seems cold, competitive, dangerous.

But this perception is not the world.

It's the wound.

Scientific Insight: The Neurobiology of Perception

- The amygdala, when hyperactivated, prioritizes fear signals, shrinking access to trust and nuance (Phelps, 2006)
- The default mode network, when dominant, increases ego-centered worry and social comparison (Raichle et al., 2001)

- Polyvagal Theory tells us that safety opens access to the social engagement system—fostering trust, openness, and connection (Porges, 2011)

Conclusion:

When we regulate, we reframe.

When we feel safe, the world changes shape.

Tool: Hostile vs. Friendly Universe Reflection

MOMENT	INITIAL INTERPRETATION	WHAT FEAR SAID	WHAT TRUST REVEALED
DIDN'T GET TEXT BACK	They're mad at me	I must have done something wrong	They were just busy. I am still safe.
UNEXPECTED CHANGE AT WORK	I'm being punished	I can't trust anyone	This opens a door I hadn't seen yet.

Practice Prompt:

Where am I still filtering the world through fear?

What might I see through the lens of remembering?

Living in a Friendly Universe Means…

- You trust yourself to respond, not react
- You believe people are doing the best they can
- You're no longer attached to being right—only aligned
- You release control and choose curiosity
- You become available for love, creativity, and joy

Modality Integration

- ACT teaches us to welcome uncertainty while choosing values

- Mindfulness helps us observe fear without fusing with it

- IFS shows that when the Self leads, parts don't need to protect

- Neuroplasticity research proves: new thought patterns create new emotional experiences (Doidge, 2007)

Practice: Reframing the Day

Each evening, choose one event that felt stressful.

Ask:

1. What did fear make this mean?

2. What did love, trust, or remembering have to say instead?

3. How did this moment guide me back to myself?

Repeat for 21 days.

You'll begin to see the world differently—not because it changed, but because you did.

Integration Table

Filter	Internal State	External Interpretation	New Action
Fear	Dysregulation	I'm not safe here	Withdraw, hide
Trust	Centered presence	I am supported	Stay, engage, learn
Ego	Comparison	They're ahead of me	Overwork, shame
Soul	Rememberance	We're different	Celebrate, stay rooted

Commitment Practice: Everything Is for Me Mantra

Today, say this every time something goes wrong:

- This is for me, not against me.
- I am being shaped, not punished.
- I live in a friendly universe, and I choose to see it.

Over time, this becomes instinct.

In Summary

The world doesn't need to change.

The self does.

Not because you're broken—

but because when you remember,

you realize you were always enough.

You were always held.

You were always home.

And from this place,

life becomes a companion—

not a battle.

This is the return.

Not just to yourself,

but to the world as it truly is:

Alive. Kind. Precious. Friendly.

References

- Porges, S. W. (2011). The Polyvagal Theory.

- Doidge, N. (2007). The Brain That Changes Itself.

- Raichle, M. E., et al. (2001). A default mode of brain function. PNAS, 98(2), 676–682.

- Phelps, E. A. (2006). Emotion and cognition: Insights from studies of the human amygdala. Annual Review of Psychology, 57, 27–53.

- Hayes, S. C., Strosahl, K. D., & Wilson, K. G. (1999). Acceptance and Commitment Therapy.

Chapter 15: There Is No Failure

The Myth of Mistake, the Reality of Growth

What if everything is unfolding exactly as it should—even when it looks like it isn't?

— Karen Dubin, Ph.D., LCSW

What you are looking for is already where you are looking from.

— St. Francis of Assisi (paraphrased)

We are raised to fear failure.

To see it as proof that we are not enough.

That we are behind.

That we missed the mark.

But what if that's not true?

What if failure is not a punishment—

but a portal?

What if every wrong turn

was the exact step

you needed to take

to remember who you are?

The Dialogue

Patient: I keep replaying everything I did wrong. The relationship. The job. My past.

Clinician: When you say wrong, tell me what you mean.

Patient: I should've known better. I should've done it differently.

Clinician: And yet, here you are. More awake. More aware. Tell me if you would be here without it.

Patient: (pause) Maybe not.

Clinician: Then tell me if you think, maybe it wasn't failure. Maybe it was the way through.

Reframing Failure Through the Three Layers

Layer	What Failure Feels Like	What It Actually Is
Conscious	A wrong decision, missed goal	A call for re-alignment
Preconscious	Reinforcement of old beliefs: I'm not enough	An invitation to update the narrative
Unconscious	Shame, fear, self-sabotage	A symbolic echo asking to be seen, integrated

Scientific Insight: Growth Through Failure

- The brain learns through error: prediction error strengthens learning circuits (Schultz et al., 1997)

- Post-traumatic growth: Many people report greater clarity, connection, and purpose after failure or crisis (Tedeschi & Calhoun, 1996)

- Cognitive reappraisal: Changing how we interpret events shifts mood, resilience, and neural pathways (Gross & John, 2003)

Bottom line:

Failure isn't failure unless you stop learning.

If you keep remembering, it becomes transformation.

Tool:

THE FAILURE-TO-FEEDBACK FRAMEWORK			
EVENT	WHAT I THOUGHT IT MEANT	WHAT I LEARNED INSTEAD	NEW TRUTH I CHOOSE
LOST MY JOB	I'm unreliable	That job wasn't aligned. I wasn't listening.	I am capable of trusting my timing.
DIVORCE	I failed at love	I outgrew the version of me that settled.	I am worthy of love that matches my truth.

Practice Prompt:

List the failures you still carry.

Ask: What if they were redirections?

Modality Integration

- **ACT (Acceptance and Commitment Therapy)**: Encourages moving toward values even in the face of failure

- **Narrative Therapy:** Re-authoring the story of failure to highlight strength

- **IFS (Internal Family Systems):** Identifies the part that holds shame and gives it space to speak

- **Self-compassion practice (Neff, 2003):** Shown to decrease shame and increase resilience

Practice: Letter from the Future Self

Write a letter from your wiser future self, looking back on what you now call a failure.

Start with:

You thought you had failed. But what you didn't see was…

Let the voice of remembrance take over.

Let it show you what you couldn't see before.

Then read it aloud.

Daily, if needed.

INTEGRATION TABLE

OLD STORY	WOUND	INSIGHT	INTEGRATED TRUTH
I RUINED EVERYTHING.	Shame	I did my best with what I knew.	I am still worthy.
I WASTED YEARS.	Regret	I was learning what doesn't work.	I walk with more clarity now.
I LOST MY CHANCE.	Hopelessness	Life doesn't operate in scarcity.	I am exactly where I need to be.

Commitment Practice: The Reframe Ritual

Every night, write down one thing from the day that felt like a mistake.

Then answer:

1. What was I believing in that moment?
2. What's a deeper truth I now choose to remember?
3. How can I use this as a stepping stone tomorrow?

Watch your nervous system shift.

Watch shame turn into grace.

In Summary

There is no failure.

Only forgetting.

And every time you forget—

life gives you another chance

to remember.

So rest now.

You are not behind.

You are not off-course.

You are remembering in the only way you could.

This is not the end of the story.

This is how the precious chapter begins.

References

- Schultz, W., Dayan, P., & Montague, P. R. (1997). A neural substrate of prediction and reward. Science, 275(5306), 1593–1599.

- Tedeschi, R. G., & Calhoun, L. G. (1996). The posttraumatic growth inventory. Journal of Traumatic Stress, 9(3), 455–471.

- Gross, J. J., & John, O. P. (2003). Individual differences in two emotion regulation processes. Journal of Personality and Social Psychology, 85(2), 348–362.

- Neff, K. D. (2003). The development and validation of a scale to measure self-compassion. Self and Identity, 2(3), 223–250.

- Hayes, S. C., Strosahl, K. D., & Wilson, K. G. (1999). Acceptance and Commitment Therapy.

Chapter 16: Wholeness Was Never Lost

It Was Only Forgotten

The self is not something you find. It is something you remember.

— Karen Dubin, Ph.D., LCSW

We search.

We strive.

We perform.

We break down.

We rebuild.

And one day, after all the effort—

after all the becoming—

we fall still.

And in that stillness, we hear something ancient:

You were never broken.

Not once.

Not for a moment.

Not even in the worst of it.

You only forgot your wholeness.

The Dialogue

Patient: I've spent so many years trying to fix myself.

Clinician: What if there's nothing to fix?

Patient: Then what do I do with all the pain?

Clinician: What about honoring it, letting it shape you, and not defining you? How about remembering that you are not your story, that you are the one who carries it. Whole?

What Is Wholeness?

Wholeness is not perfection.

It is not getting everything right.

It is not being untouched by trauma.

Wholeness is the capacity to hold all of it:

- The light and the shadow
- The grief and the grace
- The mistake and the miracle
- The human and the precious

It is the unwavering ground beneath all that changes.

Scientific Insight: The Brain's Default Wholeness

Even in trauma, depression, or fragmentation, the brain seeks integration:

- Neuroplasticity allows for constant reorganization (Doidge, 2007)
- Default Mode Network becomes quieter in moments of self-transcendence (Brewer et al., 2011)
- Mindfulness and compassion strengthen connectivity between emotional and rational centers (Lutz et al., 2008)

The nervous system does not long for perfection.

It longs for coherence.

And coherence is the experience of wholeness.

Tool: The Wholeness Inventory

Use this inventory to reflect on the degree to which you are living from a sense of wholeness, and identify areas where you may still be striving, fragmenting, or forgetting parts of yourself.

Instructions:

Each week, take 10–15 minutes to complete this inventory. Use it as a mirror to witness your current state, not as a tool for judgment. Circle the areas where you feel most aligned. Highlight areas that feel disconnected or fragmented. Then reflect with compassion and curiosity.

Domains of Wholeness:

1. Physical (Body Awareness, Health, Sleep, Movement)
2. Emotional (Range, Expression, Regulation, Permission to Feel)
3. Mental (Clarity, Focus, Beliefs, Inner Dialogue)
4. Relational (Connection, Boundaries, Authenticity)
5. Spiritual (Meaning, Presence, Awe, Guidance)
6. Purpose (Alignment, Contribution, Fulfillment)
7. Creative (Expression, Joy, Play, Imagination)

Reflection Questions:

- Where in my life do I feel most whole?
- What part of me do I tend to forget or leave behind?
- What helps me feel most integrated?
- What small act can I take this week to honor one part of myself I've neglected?

Weekly Wholeness Self-Check (1–10 Scale):

Rate each domain above on a scale of 1 to 10 for how aligned and whole you feel in that area. Track patterns and trends over time to help guide your self-remembrance journey.

AREA OF LIFE	WHAT I THOUGH WAS BROKEN	WHAT I NOW SEE AS WHOLE	REMINDERR
EMOTIONS	Too Sensitive	Deeply Attuned	My sensitivity is a gift
PAST DECISIONS	Regrets	Lessons in Disguise	I did what I could with what I knew
BODY	Flaws, Illness	Messenger and Protector	My body remembers—and heals

Practice Prompt:

What if I don't need to be healed…

but witnessed?

Modality Integration

- Gestalt Therapy: Embraces all parts as belonging

- IFS (Internal Family Systems): Restores internal balance through the Self's leadership

- Compassion-Focused Therapy: Helps us approach our suffering with warmth instead of judgment

- Mindfulness-Based Practices: Anchor the experience of observing wholeness without needing to change the moment

Practice: Speak to the Forgotten Part Ritual

1. Sit quietly.

2. Identify the part of you that feels broken.

3. Speak to it from your remembered self:

   a. You are not broken.

   b. You were trying to keep me safe.

   c. You belong. You are part of the whole.

4. Place your hand over your heart. Breathe.

Repeat daily for 7 days.

Notice the shift.

INTEGRATION TABLE

BELIEF FROM FORGETTING	RESULT	REMEMBERED TRUTH	NEW WAY OF BEING
I'M BROKEN	Shame, Isolation	I am whole and human	Self-compassion
SOMETHING IS MISSING IN ME	Overcompensating	I already contain what I seek	Grounded confidence
I HAVE TO FIX MYSELF	Exhaustion	I need only to return to myself	Restful awareness

Commitment Practice: Mirror of Wholeness

Each morning, look in the mirror and say aloud:

- I am whole.

- Even when I forget, I am whole.

- There is nothing wrong with me. There never was.

End each statement with a full breath in... and out.

In Summary

You are not on a journey to be good enough.

You are on a journey to remember:

You always were.

Your wounds are real—

but they are not the whole story.

Your mistakes happened—

but they are not your identity.

Your wholeness is not a reward.

It is your birthright.

And it has been waiting.

Quietly.

Patiently.

Lovingly.

For your return.

References

- Doidge, N. (2007). The Brain That Changes Itself.

- Brewer, J. A., et al. (2011). Meditation experience is associated with differences in default mode network activity and connectivity. PNAS, 108(50), 20254–20259.

- Lutz, A., et al. (2008). Attention regulation and monitoring in meditation. Trends in Cognitive Sciences, 12(4), 163–169.

- Gilbert, P. (2009). The Compassionate Mind.

- Schwartz, R. C. (2001). Internal Family Systems Therapy.

Chapter 17: The World Within

From Self-Improvement to Self-Remembrance

You do not become good by trying to be good, but by finding the goodness that is already within you.

— Eckhart Tolle

We live in a culture of self-improvement.

Fix this. Heal that. Upgrade everything.

We treat the self like a project.

As if one more journal, one more course, one more ritual will finally make us... enough.

But what if self-improvement is not the path?

What if it's a distraction?

What if the way forward isn't up—

but in?

Because underneath the fixing, the striving, the trying—

there is a truth waiting quietly:

You were never meant to improve yourself.

You were meant to remember yourself.

The Dialogue

Patient: I've done everything—therapy, retreats, shadow work, affirmations—and I still feel like something's missing.

Clinician: And tell me what you think that something is.

Patient: (quietly) Me. I think I've been trying so hard to be better, I forgot how to just be.

Clinician: That's not failure. That's arrival.

Self-Improvement vs. Self-Remembrance

Self Improvement	Self Rememberance
Strives to Change	Sits With What Is
Seeks to Become	Sees What's Already There
Fixes from Fear	Acceps With Self-Compassion
Adds Layers	Peeks Them Away
Feels like Work	Feels Like Homecoming

Key Insight:

Self-improvement often arises from a conditioned self that believes worth must be earned.

Self-remembrance is the work of the authentic self—the one who knows it already belongs.

Scientific Insight: The Power of Self-Acceptance

- Self-compassion is more strongly linked to emotional resilience than self-esteem (Neff, 2003)

- Experiential acceptance reduces stress and improves mental flexibility (Hayes et al., 2006)

- The default mode network quiets when we are in a state of present-centered acceptance—supporting connection, creativity, and inner peace

The brain doesn't need us to be perfect.

It needs us to feel safe enough to be honest.

Tool:

The Self-Remembrance Inventory

AREA OF LIFE	WHAT I TRIED TO IMPROVE	WHAT I CHOOSE TO REMEMBER	DAILY ANCHOR
CONFIDENCE	Forced positive affirmations	I am enough when I am real	Breathing into self-trust
RELATIONSHIPS	Tried to be less much	I am worthy of being seen fully	Saying what I need, softly

Practice Prompt:

What have I been trying to fix about myself that is actually a forgotten truth waiting to be seen?

Modality Integration

- Mindfulness-Based Cognitive Therapy (MBCT): Reframes self-judgment into observation

- **ACT (Acceptance and Commitment Therapy):** Moves from avoidance to meaningful presence

- **IFS (Internal Family Systems):** Allows inner parts to be remembered, not eliminated

- **Existential Therapy:** Grounds the self in meaning, responsibility, and choice—not perfection

Practice: The Remembrance Mirror

Each morning, look into a mirror and say:

- I'm not here to become someone else.

- I'm here to be fully myself.

- I release fixing. I welcome remembering.

- Nothing is missing. I return to who I am.

Hold your gaze with tenderness.

Let this be enough.

INTEGRATION TABLE

FIXING MINDSET	DRIVING EMOTION	REMEMBERED SHIFT	NEW WAY OF BEING
I MUST BE MORE SUCCESSFUL	Insecurity	Success if alignment.	I act from values, not fear
I HAVE TO HEAL THIS PART OF ME	Shame	This part needs compassion.	I sit with, not silence, it
IF I IMPROVE ENOUGH, I'LL BE LOVED	Fear of Rejection	I am already lovable	I express instead of perform

Commitment Practice: Stop Fixing Journal

Each evening this week, write:

- What did I try to fix about myself today?

- How did that effort feel—empowering or exhausting?

- What did I forget about my wholeness in that moment?

- What do I choose to remember tomorrow?

Watch the shift.

In Summary

The world doesn't need a better version of you.

It needs a truer version.

Your healing doesn't come from control.

It comes from return.

Return to the stillness beneath striving.

Return to the truth beneath performance.

Return to the self who was never lost—only layered over.

You are not a problem to be solved.

You are a presence to be remembered.

References

- Neff, K. D. (2003). The development and validation of a scale to measure self-compassion.

- Hayes, S. C., et al. (2006). Acceptance and commitment therapy: Model, processes and outcomes.

- Segal, Z. V., et al. (2018). Mindfulness-Based Cognitive Therapy for Depression.

- Schwartz, R. C. (2001). Internal Family Systems Therapy.

- Yalom, I. D. (1980). Existential Psychotherapy.

Chapter 18: Love as the Final Memory

The Origin, the Return, the Whole of Who We Are

Love is the bridge between you and everything.
— Rumi

There is a moment in every true healing journey—

a quiet, precious moment—

when something deeper than words emerges.

It's not another insight.

Not another breakthrough.

Not another diagnosis.

It's a feeling so familiar…

so ancient…

so obvious once you touch it—

Love.

The kind that existed before you were born.

The kind that held you when no one else did.

The kind that still pulses, even when you forget.

The Dialogue

Patient: So much of my life has been about trying to be loved.

Clinician: What if love isn't something you earn, but something you are?

Patient: But I've done so much I'm not proud of.

Clinician: And love was still there. Watching. Waiting. Never leaving.

Patient: (softly) That's what I feel now. Like something always loved me. Even when I didn't love myself.

Clinician: That's the final remembering.

Why We Forget Love

- Because we learned love was conditional
- Because we were taught love had to be earned
- Because love got tangled with pain, control, absence
- Because the world told us we had to deserve it

But real love is not a transaction.

It is a truth.

And once we touch that truth,

nothing is ever the same.

Scientific Insight: Love and the Brain

- Love activates the ventromedial prefrontal cortex, associated with safety, empathy, and reward
- Oxytocin, the love hormone, reduces amygdala activity and lowers stress
- Compassion meditation increases gray matter in regions tied to connection (Lutz et al., 2008)
- Feeling loved—even just imagining it—regulates blood pressure, improves immune function, and reduces inflammation

Love doesn't just heal the heart.

It rewires the brain.

It recalibrates the body.

It remembers the soul.

Tool: The Love Memory Map

This tool is designed to help you trace, explore, and rediscover the places, people, and moments where you felt the presence of love most vividly. By mapping these moments, you can begin to see the patterns and reawaken your connection to love as a lived memory, not just a concept.

Instructions

1. Find a quiet space. Center yourself with three slow, deep breaths.

2. Close your eyes and bring to mind a moment in your life when you felt loved — truly, wholly, unconditionally loved.

3. Now open your eyes and begin to journal freely in response to the prompts below.

The Love Memory Map Prompts

- What was the moment? Where were you?

- Who was there with you (if anyone)?

- How did your body feel in that moment?

- What thoughts or beliefs did you hold about yourself in that moment?

- If that moment had a color, what would it be?

- What emotions were present?

- What does that memory teach you about what love means to you?

Reflect and Reintegrate

Once you have mapped at least three love memories, take a moment to reflect:

- What do they have in common?

- Where do you notice love showing up most naturally in your life?

- What do these memories reveal about how you give and receive love today?

- How can you anchor yourself in these memories to live more from love?

Commitment Practice

Each morning for the next week, revisit one of these memories. Let it guide your intentions for the day. Ask yourself:

- What would it look like to live from this memory today?

- Who in my life could benefit from this love?

- How do I honor this memory in my present choices?

WHEN I FELT IT	WHO OR WHAT GAVE IT	WHAT IT FELT LIKE	WHAT I FORGOT THEN	WHAT I REMEMBER NOW
Grandma's hug	Unconditional presence	Warmth, peace	I have to grow up fast	I was always helf
Pet as a child	Safety without words	Joy, simplicity	Love needs language	Love is presence

Practice Prompt:

Make a list of every moment you've ever felt even a flicker of love—real, safe, soft love.

Let it grow.

Then sit in silence.

Feel it return.

Modality Integration

- Loving-Kindness Meditation (Metta): Proven to increase positive emotions and reduce self-criticism

- Compassion-Focused Therapy: Helps those with shame histories reconnect with their capacity to give and receive love

- IFS (Internal Family Systems): Views the Self as inherently loving and curious

- Attachment-Based Therapy: Rebuilds the foundation for love in relationships and within the self

Practice: Return to Love Ritual

Each evening, place your hand over your heart.

Say aloud:

- I was born of love.

- I was made for love.

- Even when I forgot, love never left.

- I am remembering now.

Pause.

Feel the resonance.

Repeat until the truth lands.

INTEGRATION TABLE

THOUGHT FROM FORGETTING	FEELING	LOVE'S REFRAME	PRACTICE
NO ONE WILL EVER LOVE ME IF THEY SEE THE REAL ME.	Shame	The real me is what love is for.	Reveal something true
I RUINED EVERYTHING.	Regret	I'm still worthy of love, always.	Self-forgiveness letter
I DON'T KNOW WHAT LOVE IS.	Numbness	Love is what's left when fear dissolves.	Meta meditation

Commitment Practice: Let Love Be Enough

Today, replace striving with love.

Before every decision, every action, every response—ask:

What would love do here?

Let that be enough.

Let it guide you.

Let it return you.

In Summary

You were not born to chase love.

You were born to be it.

And every moment of shame, pain, loss, and fear—

was just one more veil

to be lifted

until you could remember:

Love is not a reward.

Love is the origin.

Love is the medicine.

Love is the final memory.

And it has been waiting

in the quiet

beneath every question.

References

- Lutz, A., et al. (2008). Regulation of the neural circuitry of emotion by compassion meditation.

- Gilbert, P. (2009). The Compassionate Mind.

- Davidson, R. J., & Lutz, A. (2008). Buddha's brain: Neuroplasticity and meditation.

- Porges, S. W. (2011). The Polyvagal Theory.

- Neff, K. D., & Germer, C. K. (2013). A pilot study and randomized controlled trial of the Mindful Self-Compassion program.

Chapter 19: The Precious Pause

Living as One Who Remembers

Almost everything will work again if you unplug it for a few minutes. Including you.
— Anne Lamott

There is a moment—between breath in and breath out—

where silence lives.

Where time softens.

Where the self is no longer performing, fixing, comparing, reacting.

Just being.

Just presence.

Just remembrance.

This moment is the Precious Pause.

It is not passive.

It is not indulgent.

It is not doing nothing.

It is doing the one thing that changes everything:

Stopping long enough to remember.

The Dialogue

Patient: I get so caught up in things. Emails, people, emotions. I forget everything I've worked on.

Clinician: And when you remember—tell me what helps?

Patient: Honestly? Silence. A breath. Looking at the sky.

Clinician: That's the precious pause. It's not about controlling your life—it's about returning to it.

Why We Need the Pause

Without pausing, we:

- Live in reaction
- Get hijacked by the conditioned self
- Act from fear or habit
- Abandon the wisdom we've gained

With the pause, we:

- Return to the present
- Access the prefrontal cortex (clarity, choice)
- Reclaim authorship
- Live as one who remembers

The Precious Pause interrupts forgetting.

It is remembrance in real time.

Scientific Insight: The Neuroscience of Pausing

- Mindful pausing activates the anterior cingulate cortex (attention) and insula (self-awareness)
- Pausing reduces sympathetic nervous system activity (fight/flight) and increases parasympathetic tone (rest/restore)
- Neuroplasticity requires space—pauses give time for new neural pathways to strengthen (Doidge, 2007)

Even a 10-second pause between stimulus and response rewires your life.

Tool: The Precious Pause Method (3 Steps)

1. **STOP**

    a. Literally stop moving, talking, scrolling, planning.

2. **BREATHE**

    a. Inhale deeply through the nose (4 seconds).

    b. Hold (2 seconds).

    c. Exhale slowly through the mouth (6 seconds).

3. **REMEMBER**

    a. Ask: Who am I in this moment?

    b. What matters most right now?

    c. What would love do?

Practice Prompt: Daily Precious Pauses

Choose 3 times each day to pause intentionally:

- Morning: before reaching for your phone
- Midday: before a decision or conversation
- Evening: before going to sleep

Journal:

What did I notice when I paused?

What shifted?

What truth returned?

Modality Integration

- **ACT:** Uses mindfulness to slow down reactivity and choose values-aligned actions
- **MBSR (Mindfulness-Based Stress Reduction):** Trains the nervous system to stabilize through pause

- **Polyvagal Theory:** Emphasizes that safety is found in stillness and connection

- **Psychoanalysis:** Teaches that insight emerges in the spaces between words, not just the words themselves

INTEGRATION TABLE

TRIGGER	HABITUAL REACTION	PRECIOUS PAUSE RESPONSE	RESULT
CRITICAL EMAIL	Panic, defensivenes	Breathe. Reflect. Delay response.	Respond with clarity, not fear
ARGUMENT WITH PARTNER	Escalation	Pause. Touch heart. Soften voice.	Connection instead of conflict
OVERWHELM AT WORK	Multitasking	Close eyes. 3 breaths. Reset.	Focus, grounded action

Commitment Practice: Precious Pause Card

Write this on a card. Keep it with you:

Pause.

Breathe.

Remember.

You are not your fear.

You are not your past.

You are not alone.

You are the one who remembers.

Read it every time you forget.

In Summary

The Precious Pause is not a retreat from life—

it is a return to life.

It is the breath between forgetting and remembering.

The stillness where wholeness returns.

The space where the conditioned self dissolves…

and the true self speaks.

This is your practice now:

Not to strive.

Not to fix.

But to pause.

And in that pause,

to remember

again

and again

and again.

References

- Doidge, N. (2007). The Brain That Changes Itself.
- Kabat-Zinn, J. (1990). Full Catastrophe Living.
- Porges, S. W. (2011). The Polyvagal Theory.
- Lutz, A., et al. (2008). Attention regulation and monitoring in meditation.
- Hayes, S. C., Strosahl, K. D., & Wilson, K. G. (1999). Acceptance and Commitment Therapy.

Chapter 20: Your Life Is the Ceremony

Integration as Daily Practice

Enlightenment is when a wave realizes it is the ocean.
— Thich Nhat Hanh

We wait for precious moments.

Retreats. Rituals. Breakthroughs.

We think: That's when I'll remember.

But what if you're missing the point?

What if the precious isn't somewhere else?

What if the precious is right here?

The morning coffee.

The way you speak to yourself.

The silence between tasks.

The breath before sleep.

Your life is the ceremony.

And every moment is an altar.

The Dialogue

Patient: I feel so connected when I meditate or journal. But then the rest of my day is chaos.

Clinician: Might it be because you're making remembering an event. What if it's a way of being?

Patient: But how?

Clinician: Tell me what you think.

Patient: It's hard to tell.

Clinician: Might it be through integration? Through rhythm? Through choosing to bring the precious unto the ordinary.

Patient: (softly) I've never thought of brushing my teeth as a spiritual practice.

Clinician: What if it can be? What if It already is? If you remember.

The 4 Pillars of Daily Integration

- Ritual – Repeating small acts with intention
- Rhythm – Building consistency, not perfection
- Reflection – Staying connected to meaning
- Relationship – Bringing remembrance into how we relate to others

These are not disciplines of performance.

They are practices of presence.

Scientific Insight: Why Integration Works

- Repetition with emotional salience creates new neural wiring (Hebb's Law)
- Ritual reduces anxiety by creating predictability and perceived control (Norton & Gino, 2014)
- Small daily practices compound into long-term behavior and identity shifts (Duhigg, 2012)
- Reflective journaling increases self-awareness, coherence, and well-being (Pennebaker, 1997)

Integration is not what we do once.

It's what we return to, again and again.

Tool:

My Daily Ceremony Template			
TIME OF DAY	**PRACTICE**	**INTENTION**	**REMEMBERED PHRASE**
Morning	Hand on heart, 3 breaths	Being in presence	I am here.
Midday	Precious Pause	Regulate, reset	This moment is enough.
Evening	Gratitude Journal	Close in wholeness	Today, I returned to myself.

Practice Prompt:

Design your own 3-part daily ceremony.

Small. Simple. Repeatable.

Let it hold you.

Modality Integration

- **ACT:** Encourages values-based living, moment to moment
- **MBCT:** Uses brief mindful check-ins throughout the day
- **Narrative Therapy:** Reclaims the story through everyday language and action
- **Psychoanalytic Integration:** Honors repetition as the space where the unconscious becomes conscious

Practice: The One-Moment Ritual

Choose one daily activity (brushing teeth, opening email, walking).

Before or during it, say:

- This is precious.
- This is part of my remembering.
- Even now, I am whole.

The action becomes a mirror.

And life becomes a living altar.

INTEGRATION TABLE: LIVING REMEMBERANCE			
LIFE DOMAIN	**OLD HABIT**	**NEW RITUAL**	**MEANING**
MORNINGS	Scroll phone	Light candle, breathe	Begin with intention
WORK	React to stress	Pause + Statement	Anchor to self
RELATIONSHIPS	People-please	Express true need	Honor truth
BODY	Ignore fatigue	Touch, rest, hydrate	Remember worth

Commitment Practice: Ceremony Tracker

For the next 7 days, track:

- One precious pause
- One intentional act
- One self-honoring choice
- One truth remembered

At the end of each day, ask:

Did I live today like it mattered?

Did I remember—at least once?

Because once is all it takes to return.

In Summary

Your life is not waiting for some future version of you to be ready.

It is precious now.

Not because of what you accomplish—

but because of how you show up.

With presence.

With kindness.

With remembrance.

Let every breath be your ritual.

Let every choice be your prayer.

Let every moment be your altar.

You don't need to escape to the precious.

You are already standing in it.

References

- Hebb, D. O. (1949). The Organization of Behavior.
- Norton, M. I., & Gino, F. (2014). Rituals alleviate grief by making people feel in control. Journal of Experimental Psychology
- Duhigg, C. (2012). The Power of Habit.
- Pennebaker, J. W. (1997). Opening Up: The Healing Power of Expressing Emotion.
- Hayes, S. C., Strosahl, K. D., & Wilson, K. G. (1999). Acceptance and Commitment Therapy.

Part V: The Secret Is in Remembering

Chapter 21: Final Words from the Soul

You Were Never Lost. You Only Forgot.

Final Words from the Soul

You thought you were here to change.
But you were here to remember.

— Mardoche Sidor, MD

There is a place inside you

that has never been afraid.

Never been lost.

Never been broken.

You don't need to find it.

You only need to pause long enough

to let it speak.

It has been whispering all along:

I am here.

I am whole.

I remember.

The Dialogue

Patient: So now what? I've remembered. I've returned. What happens next?

Clinician: Now you live from it.

Patient: But I'll forget again.

Clinician: Yes. And then you'll pause. And then you'll remember.

Patient: (smiling) So that's the real secret.

Clinician: Yes.

The secret isn't never forgetting.

The secret is always remembering.

What You've Remembered

You've remembered that healing is not linear.

That truth lives beneath the noise.

That failure is an invitation.

That your body is wise.

That your patterns have roots.

That your story is precious.

That love was always there.

That your presence is enough.

You've remembered that wholeness isn't earned—

it's reclaimed.

And that remembering happens in the breath,

in the body,

in the mirror,

in the moment.

THE FINAL INTEGRATION TABLE

LAYER	WHAT YOU REMEMBERED	HOW YOU RETURN
CONSCIOUS	I can choose presence	Precious Pause, aligned action
PRECONSCIOUS	My patterns are not who I am	Schema reflection, inner child care
UNCONSCIOUS	I am whole even in shadow	Dreamwork, free association, inner listening
TRANSPERSONAL	I chose this life to grow	Ceremony, awe, stillness, soul dialogue

The Soul's Letter (Write Your Own)

Begin like this:

Dear [Your Name],

Even before you were born, I knew you.

I loved you.

I waited for the day you would remember me.

You forgot—but that forgetting was part of the journey.

Now you are awake.

Now you are walking home, even as you live this life.

Don't try so hard.

Just return.

And if you forget again… I'll still be here.

Love,

Your Soul

Read this aloud whenever you lose you forget your way.

Commitment Practice: Living as the Remembering

For the rest of your life:

- Choose presence over perfection
- Choose returning over proving
- Choose silence when you're not sure
- Choose love when you forget
- Choose pause when the noise gets loud
- Choose kindness when the shame speaks
- Choose truth when the world performs
- Choose you, exactly as you are

Because…

You are not the story.

You are the one who remembers it.

You are not the body.

You are the one who breathes through it.

You are not the fear.

You are the one who sees it arise and stay steady.

You are not becoming.

You are returning.

You are not waiting.

You are already home.

Final Reflection

You may close this book.

But you will never again

close the part of you that has remembered.

Let every day become your remembering.

Let your breath be the bridge.

Let your stillness be your compass.

Let your life become the precious path it was always meant to be.

Because in the end,

the secret is in remembering.

And now—

you remember.

References (Final Selection)

- van der Kolk, B. A. (2014). The Body Keeps the Score.

- Doidge, N. (2007). The Brain That Changes Itself.

- Porges, S. W. (2011). The Polyvagal Theory.

- Neff, K. D. (2003). The development and validation of a scale to measure self-compassion.

- Tolle, E. (2004). The Power of Now.

- Schwartz, R. C. (2001). Internal Family Systems Therapy.

- Lutz, A., et al. (2008). Regulation of the neural circuitry of emotion by compassion meditation.

Epilogue

A Return Remembered

It was never about becoming.

It was always about returning.

There are stories we've told for so long, we mistake them for truth.

Stories of what we are not.

Stories of where we went wrong.

Stories of how we must earn worthiness, love, peace.

But at some point in this journey—maybe halfway through a chapter, maybe in the silence between sessions—you paused.

And in that pause, something shifted.

You began to remember.

Not like remembering a fact.

Not like remembering a name.

But like remembering a place you've always known, even if you've never been there before.

A memory stored not in words, but in breath.

A knowing not of the mind, but of the soul.

You Were Never Lost

All this time, you've been taught to search outside.

To strive. To fix. To improve.

But this book was never an invitation to search.

It was an invitation to stop.

To turn inward.

To listen.

Because you were never broken.

You were never missing.

You simply forgot.

You searched the world for what was always within.

You climbed through suffering,

through silence,

through forgetting—

only to arrive back

at the place you never truly left.

You have called this a healing.

A transformation.

A remembering.

But the truth is simpler:

You have come home.

And home is not a place.

It is the breath you just took.

It is the stillness that holds you.

It is the self you no longer run from.

And Then, You Returned

Not to the version of you shaped by others.

Not to the identity built from survival.

But to the essence.

To the presence.

To the self that cannot be named, but can always be felt.

The one who doesn't hustle to be seen.

The one who rests inside stillness.

The one who loves without effort—because love is what you are.

There Is No Finish Line

So now, go.

Not to do more.

Not to fix anything.

But to live as one who has remembered:

That you are not the noise—

You are the quiet underneath.

That you are not the wound—

You are the witness, the wisdom, the weaver of light.

That you are not here to be better—

You are here to be whole.

There is no final arrival in this path.

Only deeper layers of remembering.

You'll forget again.

You'll stray.

You'll hear the noise of the world louder than the voice within.

But now—you know the way back.

Walk slowly.

Speak kindly.

Choose love.

Choose truth.

Choose pause.

And when the forgetting comes—

as it always will—

don't be afraid.

Just stop.

Just breathe.

Just remember.

You are the secret.

You are the remembering.

You are already home.

The path is breath.

The tool is pause.

The rhythm is presence.

The destination is… you.

A Final Whisper

You are not here to prove.

You are not here to perform.

You are here to remember.

And to live as one who remembers.

Conclusion

The Secret Is in Remembering

A Final Letter to the Reader

Dear One,

You have reached the final page—but not the end.

If you've journeyed with these words, then something in you already knew:

This was never about knowledge.

It was about remembrance.

You did not read this book to become someone new.

You read it to remember the truth you've always carried.

The voice that has always whispered.

The stillness that has always waited.

And if you take nothing else from this—take this:

You were never lost. You only forgot.

You forgot in order to survive.

You forgot because it was once safer not to know.

You forgot because the world told you what you should be, before you had time to ask who you are.

But even in the forgetting,

you left clues for yourself.

In your longing.

In your questions.

In the quiet ache that said, This isn't all of me.

That ache was your map home.

You Are the Integration

You don't need to do more to be whole.

You don't need to wait for the perfect plan, the right moment, the final healing.

You only need to pause.

To notice what's already here.

To live like someone who remembers.

Let your breath be your compass.

Let your rituals be your return.

Let your choices speak of your wholeness.

And when you forget again—and you will—

Pause.

Smile.

And begin again.

One Last Thing

If this book touched something in you, it is because that something already lived in you.

We didn't give it to you.

We simply reminded you.

So go now—not to search, but to live.

Not to earn, but to embody.

Not to become, but to remember.

You were never meant to strive for the truth.

You are the truth.

And the secret…

was always in remembering.

With love,

SWEET Institute
Karen Dubin, PhD, LCSW
Mardoche Sidor, MD

Invitation to the Reader

You Are Part of the Remembering Now

Dear Reader,

You've made it to the final page.

But the remembering continues—through you.

Every time you pause instead of perform…

Every time you speak from truth instead of fear…

Every time you live from alignment instead of survival…

You are not just remembering—you are inviting others to remember too.

This is how we shift the world.

One breath.

One moment.

One soul, remembering another.

Your Reflection

What has this book awakened in me that I don't want to forget?

Write it down.

Say it aloud.

Live it, in the smallest possible way, today.

Call to Action: Share Your Remembering

If this book spoke to you, consider doing one (or all) of the following:

- Share it. Pass it on to someone else who's ready to remember.
- Live it. Choose one practice to continue daily.

- Teach it. Use the framework with your clients, community, or family.

- Return to it. Let the pages mark your seasons of growth.

- Reflect with us. Join us at www.sweetinstitute.com

Review Request

Your voice matters.

If this book moved you, we would be deeply grateful if you'd take a moment to leave a review on Amazon, Goodreads, or wherever you found it.

Your reflection may be the mirror that helps someone else say:

Yes. I remember now.

With love and presence,

Karen & Mardoche
SWEET Institute Publishing

Final Acknowledgments

Some books are written with the hands.

This one was written with the breath.

It was whispered by memory.

Carried by longing.

And shaped by the collective ache to return to something true.

To every soul who has sat in silence, unsure of who they are—

To every healer who has dared to go inward before guiding others—

To every seeker who has asked not just what to do, but who to be—

This book is for you.

To those whose stories became precious mirrors—the clients, patients, and clinicians who have courageously shared their pain, wisdom, and wonder with us over the years—thank you for teaching us how to listen beyond the surface.

To our ancestors—known and unknown—who remind us through dreams, breath, and resonance that remembering is not a new path, but an ancient one.

To those we may never meet, whose lives this book will quietly touch—may it meet you in exactly the right moment, and may you remember what you've always known.

And to the version of ourselves who once forgot—thank you for surviving long enough to find the way back.

This is the acknowledgment not just of people,

but of presence.

Not just of effort,

but of essence.

For everything that made this book possible,

and for everything that made it necessary—

we remember you.

With devotion,

Karen & Mardoche
SWEET Institute

Reader Integration Toolkit

Purpose:

To help you move from knowing to remembering.

From remembering to living.

From living to becoming.

SECTION 1: Daily Reflection Journal

A 3-part daily prompt to anchor your day in presence and return.

Daily Reflection Journal		
TIME	**PROMPT**	**SAMPLE ENTRY**
Morning	What truth am I choosing to remember today?	I am already whole.
Midday	Where have I forgotten? How can I return now?	I've rushed through the day. I pause, I breathe.
Evening	Where did I remember today? What did it feel like?	When I looked at the trees and didn't judge myself.

Weekly Reflection:

What patterns am I beginning to shift through remembering?

SECTION 2: Precious Pause Pocket Guide

Use anytime. Anywhere. Especially when you forget.

1. STOP – Gently interrupt your momentum.
2. BREATHE – Inhale 4, hold 2, exhale 6.
3. REMEMBER – Say silently:

I am not my fear. I am not my pattern. I am the one who remembers.

Repeat as needed.

SECTION 3: Conscious–Preconscious–Unconscious Map

Conscious-Preconscious-Unconscious Map

Layer	What Lives Here	Practice	Healing Tools
Conscious	Habits, behavior, structure	Daily routine, accountability	Morning anchors, habit tracker
Preconscious	Beliefs, schemas, emotional reactions	Schema reflection, journaling	Old Story/New Truth Table
Unconscious	Repressed material, core wounds	Free association, dreamwork	Soul Dialogue, Symbol Tracing

Weekly Tracker:

- What surfaced in my conscious life?
- What emotional reaction came from my preconscious patterns?
- Did I glimpse anything from my unconscious?

SECTION 4: Memory Reframe Worksheets

Old Memory → New Meaning

MEMORY	OLD BELIEF	COMPASSIONATE REFRAME	EMBODIED ACTION
I failed at love.	I am not loveable.	I was learning boundaries.	Speak one honest need in relationship.

Use this template for at least one memory per week.

SECTION 5: Ritual Templates

Morning Mirror Practice:

- Hand over heart.
- Say:
    - I am whole.
    - I do not need to become. I only need to return.
    - Today, I live as one who remembers.

Evening Return-to-Love Ritual:

- Sit in silence.
- Recall one moment of love today.
- Whisper:
    - Even here, I am loved.
    - Even now, I remember.

SECTION 6: Weekly Integration Spiral

The Week's Spiral Journal

1. What did I experience? (Conscious)
2. What did it bring up? (Preconscious)
3. What old wound did it echo? (Unconscious)
4. What did I learn or integrate?
5. What small action will I take this week to live it?

Use each Sunday as your spiral reflection day.

SECTION 7: Soul Letter Template

Begin your letter like this:

Dear [Your Name],

I never left you. I've been here the whole time.

You forgot—and that forgetting was precious.

But look at you now. You've returned…

Write this once. Re-read often. Add to it as you grow.

SECTION 8: One-Page Remembrance Card

Print. Fold. Carry with you.

Front:

I am the one who remembers.

Back:

When I forget…

- *I pause*
- *I breathe*
- *I whisper: I am already home.*
- *I choose one act of love*
- *I begin again*

Appendix A

The Topographical Model: A Quick Reference Guide

Overview

The topographical model is a foundational framework used throughout this book and in clinical practice at the SWEET Institute. It outlines how healing and transformation occur through three psychological layers—Sigmund Freud's topographical model, with the addition of a fourth, existential layer that deepens the work beyond traditional approaches.

The Four Layers of Transformation

1. Conscious Layer

Action and Awareness

- What it includes: behaviors, habits, daily routines, choices, and deliberate thought.

- Therapeutic focus: behavior modification, mindfulness, self-care, goal-setting, new patterns.

- Tools: SMART-A goal structure, accountability, habit tracking, rituals.

- Outcome: clarity, intention, momentum, stability.

2. Pre-Conscious Layer

Beliefs and Patterns

- What it includes: automatic thoughts, emotional triggers, schemas, attachment strategies.

- Therapeutic focus: cognitive restructuring, pattern awareness, emotional literacy, inner dialogue work.

- Tools: schema mapping, parts work, corrective experiences.

- Outcome: insight, coherence, emotional fluency.

3. Unconscious Layer

Repression and Integration

- What it includes: repressed memories, hidden fears, symbolic material (dreams, body symptoms).
- Therapeutic focus: free association, dreamwork, trauma integration, guided imagery.
- Tools: story mining, art and movement, metaphor-based reprocessing.
- Outcome: deep healing, release, authenticity.

4. Existential Layer

Essence and Meaning

- What it includes: identity, purpose, values, soul, spiritual memory.
- Therapeutic focus: value alignment, identity integration, meaning-making, embodiment.
- Tools: precious questions, legacy mapping, rituals of truth, breath and presence.
- Outcome: inner peace, congruence, alignment, wholeness.

Working With the Layers in Practice

- Start with safety. Stabilize at the conscious level before diving deeper.
- Move flexibly. Healing is not linear. Use the model to identify the layer where the work is stuck.
- Honor readiness. Not all clients are ready for the unconscious or existential layers.
- Return often. Each layer offers insight at different times in life. The model is a cycle, not a checklist.

Fidelity Markers for Each Layer

Layer	Fidelity Indicators
Conscious	Client sets aligned behavioral goals; uses breath/mindful rituals
Preconscious	Patterns named; schema reframed through insight and dialogue
Unconscious	Symbolic content explored; safety maintained in regression work
Existential	Identity questions explored; presence emerges without performance

Appendix B

Worksheets and Visual Tools

These tools are designed to help readers and clinicians move from intellectual understanding to experiential integration. Each worksheet can be adapted for personal use, clinical practice, or group facilitation.

1. Daily Anchor Tracking Sheet

Use this to ground your day in your remembered identity.

Instructions: Each morning, identify a word or value you wish to live from. At night, reflect on how it shaped your day.

Date	Anchor Word	Intentional Action	How I Felt	What I Remembered

2. Layer Identification Log

Help yourself or your client locate where the healing work is currently taking place.

Prompt: Which layer is most active right now?

Layer Identification Log					
SITUATION	CONSCIOUS	PRE-CONSCIOUS	UNCONSCIOUS	EXISTENTIAL	NOTES

3. Schema Uncovering Exercise

Discover the hidden beliefs shaping your choices.

Instructions: Fill this out after a trigger or recurring emotional pattern.

- Trigger:
- Emotion:
- Automatic Thought:
- Belief underneath:
- Origin memory or life stage:
- Is it still true? What's more true now?

4. Who Am I Now? Identity Grid

Integrate change by anchoring new identity beliefs in action.

Who Am I Now? Identity Grid			
DOMAIN	OLD IDENTITY	NEW IDENTITY	DAILY ANCHOR
Self-Talk	I'm always behind	I move at the pace of truth	Morning self-affirming statement
Boundaries	I must be liked	I honor my "No"	One honest response/day

5. Precious Question Journal Prompts

Use one per day, or in session.

- Who was I before I had to protect myself?
- What does my soul already know?
- Where in my life am I still performing?
- If I could speak from pure truth today, what would I say?
- What memory feels symbolic, even if it never happened?
- What do I long to remember?

6. The Return Tracker

Notice and affirm when you're living from the remembered self.

The Return Tracker

DATE	MOMENT OF REMEMBERING	WHAT I DID DIFFERENTLY	HOW IT FELT	WHAT I LEARNED

Appendix C

The Precious Pause Practice Collection

The Precious Pause is a core practice in the journey of remembering. It creates the space between reaction and response, between habit and truth, between forgetting and awakening. This collection includes brief, repeatable practices to return to presence, identity, and alignment—anytime, anywhere.

1. The 3-Breath Pause

Use when you feel overwhelmed, disconnected, reactive, or uncertain.

1. Inhale deeply through the nose for a count of 4.
2. Hold for a count of 4.
3. Exhale through the mouth for a count of 6.
4. Repeat three times.

Anchor Statement:

In this breath, I remember.

2. The Mirror Pause

Use to reconnect with your core self.

1. Stand or sit in front of a mirror.
2. Gaze softly into your own eyes.
3. Place one hand on your heart.
4. Say: You are here. You are enough. You remember.
5. Hold your gaze and breathe into the truth of it.

(Do this for 60–90 seconds.)

3. The Precious Name Pause

Use to reclaim your truth in moments of doubt or shame.

1. Write down three words that describe your remembered self (grounded, kind, free).

2. Speak them aloud slowly, one by one.

3. After each word, pause and breathe.

4. Let each word become your name for the moment.

Example:

I am grounded.

(Pause)

I am kind.

(Pause)

I am free.

4. The Disruption Pause

Use when an old pattern is rising or when about to react from conditioning.

1. Say (silently or aloud): This is a moment of choice.

2. Ask: Who do I want to be right now?

3. Drop into your body.

4. Take one full, slow breath.

5. Choose from alignment—not from reflex.

5. The Closing the Day Pause

Use at the end of the day to integrate.

1. Sit in stillness or lie down with a hand on your heart.

2. *Ask: What part of me showed up today that I am proud of?*

3. Let one word, image, or memory rise.

4. *Whisper: Thank you. I remember.*

6. The Return Ritual

Use weekly or monthly to re-center when you've drifted.

- Light a candle or sit in symbolic stillness.
- Write or speak this self-affirming statement:

    Even when I forget, I am still me.

    Even when I drift, I can return.

    I return now—not to what I was,

    but to who I have always been.

- Breathe into your center. Begin again.

Suggested Use:

- Print these and keep them on your mirror, desk, altar, or phone.
- Use with clients at the beginning or end of session.
- Choose one per week as a theme of practice.
- Invite others to create their own Precious Pauses.

Appendix D

Visual Tools & Integration Templates

This appendix includes simplified visual frameworks and fillable integration templates that accompany the core concepts in this book. Each can be adapted for personal practice, clinical use, or group exploration.

1. The Four Layers of Remembering – Visual Model Your intern could have made any of these below into a visual:

Use this to identify where healing is currently active or needed.

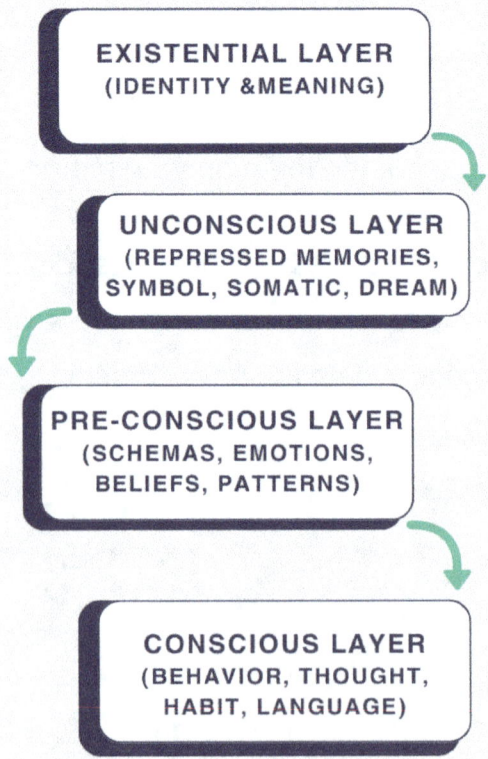

EXISTENTIAL LAYER
(IDENTITY &MEANING)

UNCONSCIOUS LAYER
(REPRESSED MEMORIES, SYMBOL, SOMATIC, DREAM)

PRE-CONSCIOUS LAYER
(SCHEMAS, EMOTIONS, BELIEFS, PATTERNS)

CONSCIOUS LAYER
(BEHAVIOR, THOUGHT, HABIT, LANGUAGE)

The 4 Layers of Remembering

2. Integration Spiral Template

Use this tool to reflect on recurring growth cycles that deepen with each remembering.

Prompt: What old situation am I experiencing from a new level of awareness?

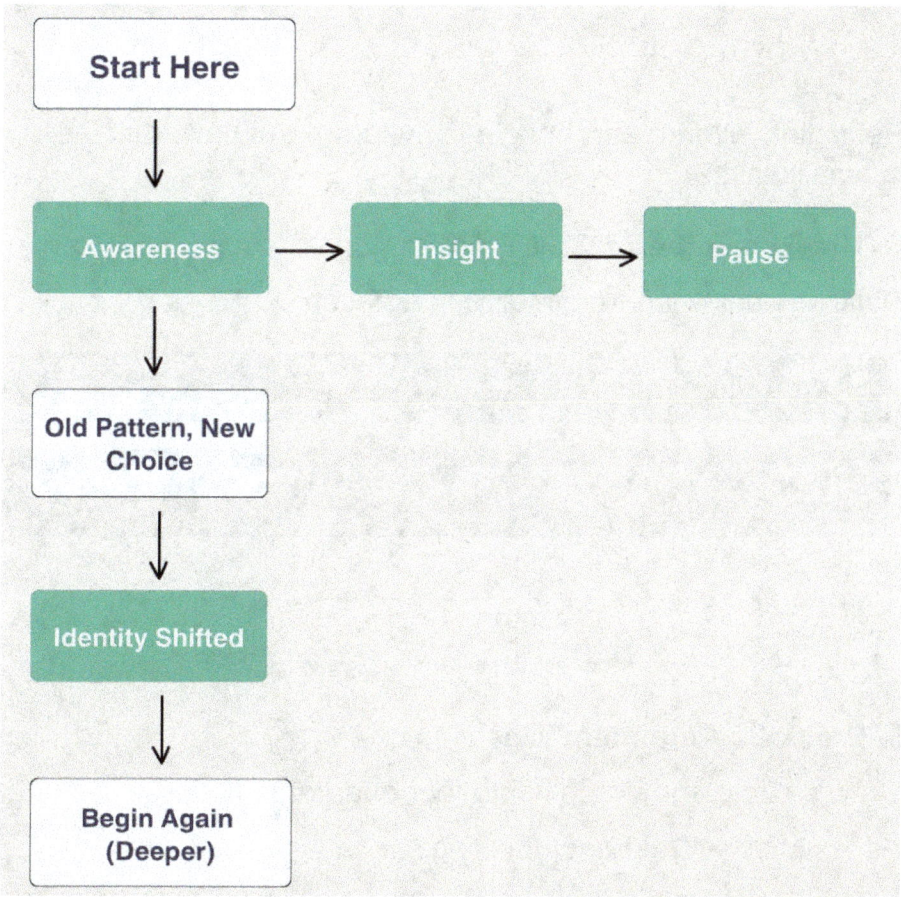

Application: Write about a moment when you noticed yourself showing up differently in a familiar situation. What changed? What did you remember?

3. Behavior → Belief → Blueprint Map

Trace a surface behavior down to a root identity script.

Behavior → Belief → Blueprint Map				
BEHAVIOR	AUTOMATIC THOUGHT	CORE BELIEF	ORIGINAL CONTEXT	NEW TRUTH

Reflection: Where can I begin to live from the new truth—even in small ways?

4. The Remembered Self Tracker

Daily or weekly log to reinforce integration.

The Remembered Self Tracker			
DATE	WHAT I DID DIFFERENTLY	HOW I FELT	WHAT THIS SAYS ABOUT WHO I AM NOW

5. Precious Alignment Wheel

Draw a circle and divide it into four quadrants:

- Mind – What am I thinking?
- Body – What am I sensing?
- Heart – What am I feeling?
- Soul – What am I knowing?

Use this check-in daily or before making big decisions. The goal is not perfection, but presence.

Clinician Note:

These tools can be printed, digitized, or used conversationally. They're designed for continuity—so remembering becomes not an event, but a way of life.

Appendix E

Training, Supervision, and Clinical Fidelity Guide

This appendix offers practical guidance for clinicians, supervisors, and facilitators who are applying The Secret Is in Remembering framework in clinical, educational, or group settings. It is designed to ensure fidelity to the model while allowing for personalization and adaptation.

1. Core Clinical Competencies

To facilitate the remembering process effectively, clinicians are to cultivate:

- **Layer Awareness**: Ability to recognize which psychological layer (conscious, pre-conscious, unconscious, existential) is active in the client's process.

- **Pacing and Permission**: Comfort in slowing down, pausing, and following the client's readiness—not urgency.

- **Presence and Self-Awareness**: Capacity to model exist-ential presence and differentiate between intervention and intrusion.

- **Integration Focus**: Shift from symptom-chasing to alignment, wholeness, and sustained rhythm.

2. Fidelity Markers for Each Layer

Fidelity Markers for Each Layer

Layer	Fidelity Indicators
Conscious	Client sets aligned behavioral goals; uses breath/mindful rituals
Preconscious	Patterns named; schema reframed through insight and dialogue
Unconscious	Symbolic content explored; safety maintained in regression work
Existential	Identity questions explored; presence emerges without performance

3. Weekly Session Template (Flexible Format)

Each session will ideally include:

1. **Opening Check-In**
   - Tell me where you are today.
   - Tell me what part of you is leading right now.

2. **Layer Clarification**
   - Identify which layer the work is happening in (explicitly or implicitly).

3. **Core Intervention or Practice**
   - Behavior change, schema work, free association, preciousnquiry, etc.

4. **Closing Integration Prompt**
   - Tell me what you remember today.
   - Tell me what you will carry with you from this session.

5. Suggested Between-Session Practice

- o A ritual, reflection, or embodied task to deepen the remembering.

4. Group Facilitation Tips

- Create psychologically safe space: ritual, rhythm, rules of resonance
- Frame each session with a theme and a layer (e.g., Today we work with unconscious symbols)
- End each session with a pause and self-affirming statement
- Invite integration, not advice-giving
- Use collective witnessing as a healing tool

5. Supervision Questions for Practitioners

- What layer are you most comfortable working in? Least comfortable?
- How do you know when a client is ready for existential work?
- What have you noticed in yourself while guiding others to remember?
- Where are you still forgetting—and how does that shape your practice?

6. Fidelity Checklist for Program Leads

At monthly or quarterly review, assess whether:

- The layered model is being consistently referenced
- Practices are applied with presence, not performance
- Clients are developing insight and identity coherence

- Clinicians are tending to their own remembering through supervision and reflection

Final Note to Facilitators:

You are not here to fix, impress, or perform.

You are here to remember alongside those you serve.

You hold the mirror—not to show others what they lack,

but to help them see what has always been there.

Recommended Reading

Books That Deepen the Journey of Remembering

Memory, Identity, and Self

- The Developing Mind by Daniel J. Siegel
- The Psychology of Life Stories by Dan P. McAdams
- Self Comes to Mind by Antonio Damasio
- The Self Illusion by Bruce Hood

Trauma, Healing, and Integration

- The Body Keeps the Score by Bessel van der Kolk
- Waking the Tiger by Peter A. Levine
- Trauma and Recovery by Judith Herman
- In an Unspoken Voice by Peter A. Levine

Existential Psychology and Meaning

- Man's Search for Meaning by Viktor E. Frankl
- The Courage to Be by Paul Tillich
- Existential Psychotherapy by Irvin D. Yalom
- The Gift of Therapy by Irvin D. Yalom
- Higher Purpose by Robert Holden

Spiritual Insight and Inner Wisdom

- The Untethered Soul by Michael A. Singer
- The Power of Now by Eckhart Tolle
- The Book of Awakening by Mark Nepo
- The Seven Spiritual Laws of Success by Deepak Chopra

- A Return to Love by Marianne Williamson

Somatic and Embodied Practice
- My Grandmother's Hands by Resmaa Menakem
- Radical Acceptance by Tara Brach
- The Wisdom of Your Body by Hillary L. McBride
- Embodied Healing by Jenn Turner

Creative and Narrative Transformation
- Writing Down the Bones by Natalie Goldberg
- The Artist's Way by Julia Cameron
- Callings: Finding and Following an Authentic Life by Gregg Levoy
- Let Your Life Speak by Parker J. Palmer

These books are not required—but they are reminders.

Of who we are.

Of what we carry.

And of the many ways we remember.

Books by the Authors

Transformational Works by Dr. Mardoche Sidor and Dr. Karen Dubin

- Time to Heal (In Print)

  A practical and poetic guide to reclaiming time, presence, and self-leadership through the 52 pillars of healing and accountability.

- Before Anything Else, Validate (In Print)

  A revolutionary framework on how validation transforms relationships, mental health care, and human connection—from the inside out.

- The Courage to Care

  Co-edited anthology of frontline clinicians who share the moments that shaped their practice, their purpose, and their humanity.

- How Life Works (In Print)

  A narrative journey through the spiritual, psychological, and scientific lessons hidden in everyday experiences.

- Reflections: The Clinician's Mirror (In Print)

  A lyrical exploration of how projection, presence, and self-awareness shape healing—from both sides of the therapy room.

- Rewriting the Script (In Print)

  A powerful guide to uncovering and releasing internalized oppression through story, identity, and spiritual liberation.

- The Kindness Imperative (In Print)

  On leadership, power, grace, and why kindness is the most transformational force we've forgotten to measure.

- The Anchor Blueprint (In Print)

  A visionary model for transforming mental health care for high-acuity populations—grounded in science, soul, and systems change.

Forthcoming Titles

- Freeing Fear
- Breaking the Pattern
- The Simplicity Principle
- Nou Se Peyi A
- Redefining Psychoanalysis

For more books and resources, visit:

www.sweetinstitutepublishing.com

About the Authors

Mardoche Sidor, M.D.

Dr. Mardoche Sidor is a quadruple-board-certified psychiatrist trained at Harvard and Columbia. He is the founder of the SWEET Institute, a global leader in transformational education for clinicians and healing professionals. With a deep commitment to bridging science and soul, Dr. Sidor has taught thousands how to move beyond symptom management and into sustained transformation.

Through his work, he helps individuals and systems remember what they once knew: that healing is not just possible—it is natural. He served as Assistant Clinical Professor of Psychiatry at Columbia University's Vagelos College of Physicians and Surgeons for eight years and is currently affiliated with the Columbia University Center for Psychoanalytic Training and Research.

Dr. Sidor serves as Medical Director of Urban Pathways and continues to mentor, teach, and lead from a place of clarity, compassion, and deep remembering.

Karen Dubin, Ph.D., LCSW

Dr. Karen Dubin is a social worker, clinical educator, and soul-centered writer who has devoted her life to the intersection of identity, healing, and wholeness. With advanced training in trauma, relational psychotherapy, and narrative practice, she brings a rare blend of academic rigor and intuitive wisdom to her work.

As co-founder and lead editor at SWEET Publishing, she helps clinicians reconnect with the heart of why they do what they do—not just as professionals, but as people on a path of remembering themselves. Her writing, teaching, and presence reflect her deep belief: We are not here to fix. We are here to return.

www.ingramcontent.com/pod-product-compliance
Lightning Source LLC
Chambersburg PA
CBHW071733120626
46550CB00002B/509